For Good or Evil

Norwegian Foreign Policy Studies No. 40

For Good or Evil

Economic Theory and North-South Negotiations

Edited by Gerald K. Helleiner

Universitetsforlaget
OSLO — BERGEN — TROMSØ

University of Toronto Press
TORONTO and BUFFALO

© Universitetsforlaget 1982
ISBN 82-00-05777-1

Published simultaneously in Canada,
the United States, the Commonwealth
except Great Britain, and Latin America
1982 by
University of Toronto Press,
Toronto and Buffalo
ISBN 0-8020-2465-3 (cloth)
ISBN 0-8020-6482-5 (paperback)

Cover design: Harald Gulli

Printed in Norway by
Nye Intertrykk as, Lommedalen

"...the ideas of economists and political philosophers, both when they are right and when they are wrong, are more powerful than is commonly understood ... soon or late, it is ideas, not vested interests, which are dangerous for good or evil."

John Maynard Keynes, *The General Theory of Employment, Interest and Money* (Harcourt, Brace and Company, New York, 1936), pp. 383-/4.

Contents

Part III
International Finance in Theory and Practice

Part IV
Economic Theory and the General Practice of International Economic Policy

Preface

Early in July, 1980, nineteen economists (listed at the end of this volume) from academic, governmental and international institutions, all of whom specialize in international and development economics, met at Refsnes Gods in Norway to consider the relevance of Western economic theories to the negotiations on a New International Economic Order. This volume contains revised versions of nine of the papers that were presented at the conference — those which I considered to be most directly addressing its subject, and which were not to be published elsewhere. They are preceded by my attempt to synthesize and summarize, in a highly personalized fashion, the three days of discussion.

As chairman of the conference, and on behalf of its members, I should like to thank those who made it possible: the Royal Ministry of Foreign Affairs of Norway, the Norwegian Institute of International Affairs, and the German Marshall Fund of the United States; its organizers: Valter Angell, John Cuddy and Per Haugestad; and Mrs. Laila Langberg of the Norwegian Institute for her organizational support. It is in the nature of our subject that they will have to wait for some time in order to see whether their efforts are rewarded.

Gerald K. Helleiner
Toronto, March 1981

List of Contributors

Edmar Lisboa Bacha is a Professor of Economics at the Catholic University of Rio de Janeiro. A Yale University Graduate, he has held research positions at MIT and Harvard. Jointly with L. Taylor, E. Cardoso, and F. Lysy, he recently published *Models of Growth and Distribution for Brazil* (Oxford University Press, 1980). Forthcoming in Portuguese is his intermediate macroeconomics textbook for semi-industrialized countries, *Análise Macroecônomica: Una Perspectiva Brasileira* (Department of Economics, Catholic University of Rio de Janeiro, 1981).

John D.A. Cuddy, a Canadian, is Chief, Quantitative Analysis Unit, Commodities Division, UNCTAD and Professor, The Graduate Institute for International Studies, Geneva. He has published actively, especially in the field of international commodity policy. He is closely identified with the newly-negotiated Common Fund for Commodities.

Carlos F. Diaz-Alejandro, is Professor of Economics at Yale University, where he teaches international trade and finance, economic development and economic history of Latin America. He has written books and articles on these subjects.

Ricardo Ffrench-Davis, is Senior Researcher and Director of the Corporación de Investigaciones Económicas para Latinoamérica (CIEPLAN) in Chile. He has taught at universities in Chile and the University of Boston, and was visiting Fellow at St. Antony's College, Oxford. He is the author of *Economía Internacional: teorías y políticas para el desarrollo,* Fondo de Cultura Económica, 1979, and co-editor of *Latin America and the New International Economic Order,* Macmillan, 1981. He has published other books and articles on international economics, Chile's economic policies, and Latin American economic development.

Gerald K. Helleiner is a Professor of Economics at the University of Toronto. His recent publications include *International Economic Disorder: Essays in North-South Relations* (Macmillan and University of Toronto, 1981); *Intra-firm Trade and the Developing Countries* (Macmillan and St. Martin's, 1981); and editing of *A World Divided, The Less Developed Countries in the International Economy* (Cambridge, 1976).

Richard Jolly, an economist, has been Director of the Institute of Development Studies at the University of Sussex. His professional life has been spent partly in research on developing countries and partly in operational work and development planning. In 1978, he worked in the OECD as special consultant on North-South issues to the Secretary-General. His recent publications include co-editing and contributing to *Redistribution with Growth, Third World Employment, Disarmament and World Development,* and an article on the nature of rich country interests in Third World development in *The World Economic Order: Past and Prospects,* edited by Sven Grassman and Erik Lundberg.

Alfred Maizels has been working on problems of development of underdeveloped countries and the associated issues of international remedial policies for the past 25 years, first as Senior Research Officer at the National Institute of Economic and Social Research, London, and then at UNCTAD, Geneva. At present he is undertaking research in this field at University College, London as well as being a consultant to the UNCTAD Commodities Division.

Stein Rossen is a senior Research Fellow at the Chr. Michelsens Institute, Bergen, Norway. Most of his professional life has been spent with the United Nations. He has been Director of the Research Division of the Economic Commission for Africa and the Economic Commission for Europe, and from 1970 to 1979 he was Deputy Secretary-General of the UNCTAD.

Frances Stewart is a Fellow of Somerville College, and Senior Research Officer, Institute of Commonwealth Studies, Oxford. She is the author of *Technology and Underdevelopment* (Macmillan, 1977) and at present is Consultant to the Centre for Research on the New International Economic Order, Oxford, on international monetary reform.

John Williamson, currently Senior Fellow at the Institute for International Economics, Washington, D.C., was recently a Professor of Economics at the Pontificia Universidade Catolica de Rio de Janeiro, was educated at LSE and Princeton and previously held positions at the Universities of York and Warwick, in the British Treasury and at the IMF. His publications, largely in the area of international monetary economics, include *The Failure of World Monetary Reform, 1971-74* (Nelson and NYU Press) and *Exchange Rate Rules: The Theory, Performance and Prospects of the Crawling Peg* (Macmillan, 1981).

Abbreviations

ACP	African Caribbean Pacific
CET	Common External Tariff
Comecon	Council for Mutual Economic Cooperation
DAC	Development Assistance Committee
DC	Developing Countries
DME	Developed Market Economies
ECDC	Economic Cooperation among Developing Countries
EEC	European Economic Community
EFTA	European Free Trade Area
ECSS	Executive Committee in Special Session
GATT	General Agreement on Tariffs and Trade
GSP	Generalized System of Preferences
IBRD	International Bank for Reconstruction and Development (World Bank)
ICID	Independent Commission on International Development
ILO	International Labour Organization
LDC	Less Developed Countries
MTN	Multilateral Trade Negotiations
NIC	Newly Industrialized Countries
NIEO	New International Economic Order
ODA	Official Development Assistance
OECD	Organization for Economic Cooperation and Development
OPEC	Organization of Petroleum Exporting Countries
SDR	Special Drawing Rights
TNC	Trans National Corporation
UN	United Nations
UNCTAD	United Nations Conference on Trade and Development
UNDP	United Nations Development Program
UNIDO	United Nations Industrial Development Organization

Chapter 1

Introduction

*Gerald K. Helleiner**

North-South dialogue, stalemate and economic theory

During the course of the 1970s, spokesmen for the developing countries placed a series of proposals for international economic and political reform upon the agenda of the United Nations and its member organizations. Their proposals for a New International Economic Order have been debated at great length at innumerable conferences within the United Nations system and elsewhere, and have been the object of negotiations in a wide variety of different fora. Among other objectives, the proposed New International Economic Order (NIEO) involves: the regulation and stabilization of international primary commodity markets and the creation of a Common Fund for this and other purposes; improved access to Northern markets for the exports of Southern countries and appropriate adjustments in Northern economies to facilitate the expansion of Southern shares of global manufacturing industry; international monetary reform; the regulation of the activities of transnational corporations and the creation and enforcement of a code of conduct governing the international transfer of technology; the promotion of economic cooperation among developing countries; increased resource flows to developing countries; and, in general, the alteration of existing institutional mechanisms and structures so as to support the objectives of devel-

* This introduction is a highly personal and impressionistic one. It does not purport to summarize the content of the papers or the discussions of the conference. Nor does it commit any of its participants to any of the views here expressed. While I have stolen freely from the ideas which others expressed during the conference, and I should like to thank all of the participants for these parts of my further education, all are absolved totally from any responsibility for the contents of this paper. So are all those who commented on an earlier draft: H.E. English, Richard Jolly, Alfred Maizels, Gus Ranis, John Sheahan, Frances Stewart, and John Williamson. Special thanks are due to John Cuddy who drafted parts of the middle section; but he, too, must be relieved of any responsibility for the final product.

opment in the Third World. Much more than in previous decades the developing countries' pressure in the 1970s has been directed to reforming the institutional framework and the "rules of the game", both in the private sector and in respect of intergovernmental agreements.

Although a consensus resolution expressing support for the concepts of the NIEO was adopted by the Sixth Special Session of the United Nations, the countries of the North have never accepted the details of the proposed reform programme. Rather, they have stalled the discussions at almost every turn, giving ground only when — as in the case of the Common Fund — the original proposal had been gradually negotiated into something quite different from that with which the South had begun, or when — as in the case of the revised guidelines for the application of IMF conditionality in its upper credit tranche lending policies — they still retained firm control over the institutions and policies at issue. North-South stalemate in the development of the NIEO programme is regarded by many policy-makers in the North as evidence of foreign policy "success".

The North-South dialogue of recent years is about specific changes in the functioning of international institutions and the rules of the present and emerging international game; it is *not* about alternative visions of "another development". No doubt the required changes in underlying theories and perceptions for the purpose of pursuing the wider objectives of improving human society in many more dimensions would be much greater than those in the fairly narrowly defined economic ones which are to be discussed in this volume.

On part of the discussion of the "quality" of development, however, there has been substantial emphasis placed by protagonists in the North-South debates. Northern policy-makers have consistently expressed their concern over the distribution of the benefits from international reforms, and have sought proof that increased Southern receipts or earnings, from whatever source, would raise the incomes of the poorest people. It would be idle to pretend that one could know that extra incomes earned by Southern actors would necessarily raise the incomes of the poor. But the inability to prove what the ultimate effects of international resource transfers or reforms would be cannot legitimately be employed as a rationale for inaction and the maintenance of the *status quo*. Certainly we need to know more about the complex interactions through which changes in one part of an interdependent system generate changes in other parts; but, while such investigations are pursued one must proceed on the basis of presumptions. "Presumption" might in this context be taken as a synonym for "frame of reference" or "implicit model". The South's policy-makers presume that international reforms will raise the incomes of the poor; Northerners have been increasingly sceptical in this regard.

(i) Economic Theory and the Analysis of North-South Issues

The NIEO debates are conducted primarily in terms of the arguments of economics. While there are unquestionably wider issues at stake in intergovernmental negotiations and "issue linkage" among them all certainly exists, the basis questions debated in this sphere of international interaction are economic ones. Those called upon to prepare briefing papers are typically economists, and, when governments have them at their disposition, so are the negotiators themselves.

There are many possible explanations for Northern opposition to the details of the South's programme for a NIEO. Our concern here is with the Northern arguments against it, which have been couched in terms of the language of economics. This volume attempts to assess the descriptive accuracy of the economic theory employed in the current North-South debates, and the effects of its use for policy prescription. The inherent logic of economic arguments is not at issue; on its own grounds, only in rare instances can it be faulted. Rather, such matters as the suitability of its premises, the relationship of its "stylized facts" to reality, and its capacity to explain and predict are the objects of our enquiry. A particular watch is kept for gaps and biases which it might be possible to repair, and there is concern throughout to improve understanding of the issues involved. In any such assessment it is virtually impossible to retain total objectivity. The hold of our conceptual frameworks is difficult to break. In the words of John Maynard Keynes, "The difficulty lies, not in the new ideas, but in escaping from the old ones, which ramify, for those of us brought up as most of us have been, into every corner of our minds". (General Theory, Preface).

World society and the world economy are highly complex. In order to try to reduce the complex reality into intelligible terms, men construct their own simplified models as to how the world works. Some models are taught in universities' social science courses. Others are developed by formally unschooled men and women who, though they do not call them "models", nevertheless construct them from their own daily experiences. The former are much more likely to be formalized and explicit in their assumptions; but the implicit model

3

upon which the Third World farmer bases his daily decisions may be just as realistic and sometimes an even better predictor of events. Underlying "models" or "theories" or "visions" of how the world functions or ought to function play important roles in men's behaviour. Religion, ideology, science and culture may all be inputs to individuals' perceptions of the world, together with a variety of individual personality traits, experiences, and hunches. Rarely is anyone so rational and consistent as to be able to relate *all* his thought or behaviour to one such underlying model; but some such model does generate presumptions as to how he will respond, at least in general terms, to particular situations.

Economics is taught not only as a positive or descriptive science but also as a normative policy-oriented one. By mastering a set of theoretical models, a collection of logical and statistical tools, and a certain body of facts and knowledge, the student of economics is encouraged to believe that it is possible to develop economics-based policy recommendations on virtually any subject, whether it is primarily an economic one or not. The structure of modern economic thought is internally consistent, amenable to adaptation in many different directions, and a powerful aid to logical analysis of economic questions. Its very rigour and power sometimes seduce those who employ it into the belief that political balances and compromises, achieved through bargaining processes rather than "the laws of economics", are contrary to nature and to be deplored.

Economic theory is typically written and taught in terms of a cautious step-by-step approach in which all of the assumptions are carefully specified and all of the resulting qualifications are noted. "Exceptional cases" are enjoyed and paradoxes abound. On the frontiers of the discipline, vigorous experimentation can be found in the juggling of assumptions, the empirical testing of hypotheses, and the adaptation and improvement of both theoretical and quantitative economic models. Once in the difficult world of policy formation, however, students of economics are prone to forget all the qualifications and assumptions, and frequently apply instead the simplest and crudest versions of the models they were taught, using, as they would put it, only "the basic principles". They are not necessarily to be blamed for this. Even eminent theorists have been seen, when pressed, to act similarly in order to be able to reach any real-world conclusions at all.

If this process of bowdlerization takes place, however, and some would argue that it is absolutely inevitable that it does, it becomes crucial to understand the sequences and models through which the subject of economics is typically taught. What are the crude models which are most likely to be retained? What does the loss of the qualifications and refinements do to the reality of the model and its capacity to facilitate understanding? Does the failure to employ the whole range of the relevant literature result in significant error or bias, and, if the latter, does it operate consistently in predictable directions? A further major question — to be addressed later — is whether existing theory, even in its most sophisticated versions, adequately represents or explains the real world.

One of the certain consequences of the use of crude theory is the tendency to apply "standard recipes" to all situations that appear roughly similar. More generally, it can result in "knee-jerk" responses and almost "intuitive" reactions to quite complex phenomena, which really require more detailed analysis. The underlying frame of reference sets a "mood" or a "tone" to discussion of economic issues.

The "theory" which lies behind dominant Northern approaches to North-South economic disputes is that of orthodox neoclassical economics. Although the modern literature of economics is rich in adaptations and elaborations of the core of the neoclassical "paradigm", many of which attempt to bring it into closer touch with reality, it is its "core" which exercises dominant influence. That core is based upon the assumption of individual, rational, and well-informed actors interacting upon competitive markets in pursuit of their own self-interest. Buyers and sellers do not transact with one another unless there is gain to both parties. From this it follows that the institution of the market is essentially benign in that it permits economic actors to achieve levels of welfare which would have been unattainable in their isolation from one another. It can be demonstrated that, under certain assumptions, the pursuit of individual self-interest will lead to the greatest possible increase in overall welfare consistent with the requirement that no actor be made any worse off than he was before entering the market. That is, scarce resources are allocated with the greatest possible efficiency among the alternative possible uses which the various market transactors collectively demand. These harmonious results are inhibited only by "market imperfections", elements of reality which are not in keeping with the assumptions of the model, and cases of "market failure", which are treated as special cases, exceptions to the general rule. The distribution of income is treated independently of the "primary" question of allocative efficiency in this approach, although it clearly affects the total composition of demand and is itself affected by the allocation of resources.

Approaching economic problems from a theoretical core of this character accustoms the analyst to treating important elements of reality, such as oligopoly, transnational corporate intra-firm trade, or imperfect and asymmetrically available information, as mere "wrinkles" on the "general case". Similarly, such difficulties of real world markets as externalities, instabilities, and "crises" are considered as oddities. The problem is not that there is no literature on these matters (in fact there is a very vigorous one); rather, it is that habits of thought develop which generate simple, and almost subconscious and automatic, approaches to economic issues which (as the relevant theoretical literature demonstrates) are far more complex than the crude core model would suggest. Almost imperceptibly, prisoners of their own paradigm, students of economics risk beginning to regard all governmental policies as "interventions", likely to impede the harmonious functioning of markets; and to regard the distribution of income (and power) as a matter wholly independent of market functioning, to be handled by separate policies (lump-sum transfers) which do not "interfere" with markets. Academic economists will instantly deny that they could be so vulgar in their application of their theories. But practitioners, who frequently have neither the time nor the inclination for the pursuit of the finer points of theory, are primarily interested in "the large picture". They need "rules of thumb"; they read only the conclusions of complex background papers; they must develop a much-simplified "frame of reference" for their daily round of dealing with specifics.

In domestic economic policy, the power of the crude underlying model to influence policy-makers has been tempered by the exigencies of politics. In the modern Western mixed economy there is substantial governmental participation in consumption, production, and rule-making. Governmental policies to influence the distribution of income, the location of industry, the level of competition and the overall behaviour of economic actors are commonplace. Allocative and distributional outcomes are arrived at through a complex mixture of social bargaining, political processes, and markets. Policy-makers employ implicit "rules of thumb" in which these various influences figure prominently, and economists are frequently derided as "too theoretical" and inadequately aware of the political determinants of action. Individual policy-makers are obviously much affected by

6

their own immediate socio-political environment. It is therefore not surprising that Scandinavian or Dutch perceptions of North-South issues are not typically so based upon market models or theory as are those of the U.S. or the Federal Republic of Germany, since the relative role of markets as against non-market institutions is smaller, at least in public perceptions if not necessarily in practice, in the former countries' polities than in those of the latter.

Of course, alternative non-market models of politico-economic relationships have also been constructed. Distribution of wealth and power can be placed, after all, at the very centre of one's concerns, with such questions as allocative efficiency and market functioning relegated to the status of the relatively unimportant "wrinkles". It is also possible to focus upon systemic changes and the longer sweep of history, in which case primary focus may be placed upon signs of systemic malfunctioning and breakdown. The "knee-jerk" responses of those whose underlying models are such non-market ones can be every bit as predictable, and their "recipes" just as monotonously "standardized", as are those of the Western policy-makers who are the primary object of our attention.

The nature of the underlying models affects the statistics that are assembled and the bases on which performance is assessed. The way in which the value of production is "added up" in order to measure the gross national product, for instance, is the product of the underlying theory, and the resulting aggregate (GNP) has been enormously influential as a measure of progress. Until very recently, on the other hand, statistics of income distribution were virtually non-existent, and assessments of progress on this front consequently almost impossible. It would be difficult not to attribute at least some of this statistical imbalance to the intellectual segmentation of these issues which is found in traditional neoclassical economic thought. Similarly, measures of the degree of market concentration in individual world markets or the degree of internalization of international trade are scarce, whereas data on the commodity composition of national exports and imports are available in enormous detail. Again, this imbalance must be at least partially attributable to the literature's fixation with explaining patterns of international trade, under competitive market assumptions, rather than assessing the distribution of its benefits or its actual overall efficiency.

(ii) *Wider Northern Perceptions of North-South Issues*

The *overall* politico-economic "frame of reference" which Northern policy-makers employ seems to rest, implicitly, upon the views that: (i) the global economy, run as it is on a more or less *laissez-faire* basis, under the aegis of the Bretton Woods institutions and the GATT, functions reasonably effectively and requires no further "global management" except when special circumstances so demand; (ii) the South is not a sufficiently important component of the global economy for it to play any greater role in global decision-making than it now does; (iii) the most important influences upon Northern welfare are those which are determined by North/North (including East/West) agreements or disputes; and (iv) the South can and should therefore be handled — as distribution is handled in traditional market theory — as a separate matter for independent bargaining over distribution, with the clear presumption that how much the Southern "clients" receive is a matter for the Northern "patrons'" discretion. (For a lucid summary of these approaches, see Hansen, 1979.) When and if particular parts of the South become sufficiently important, through their own efforts, to merit inclusion, they can be admitted to the councils of the North as junior partners, provided that they subscribe to the same rules as all the rest of the members of the "club". (The division of the world for analytical purposes into "the North" and "the South" is obviously not always the most helpful simplification.) There is no need, in the meantime, to alter the functioning of global markets or other institutions because of the clamouring of the South. Southerners are perfectly welcome to develop their own rules, and to go "collectively self-reliant", in most areas, precisely because whatever they do is seen to be of such relative insignificance to the North.

This overall perception has clearly been shaken in the special case of petroleum. And some would say that it is also at risk in respect of such issues as population, environment, and nuclear proliferation. But the linkage between these issues and the rest of the NIEO agenda, despite strenuous efforts, has still been only imperfectly made. (The most effective recent attempt to draw the arguments in respect of these "issue linkages" together for Northern audiences is the report of the Brandt Commission, but it has not yet registered any palpable impact upon underlying Northern "frames of reference".) Northern policy-makers treat and prefer to treat petroleum as a special case upon which a separate bargain can be struck. In this single case they clearly accept a conflict and bargaining model of global realities, rather than leaving the outcome to a benign and harmonious world market. Beyond the level of rhetoric they do not honestly see any serious link between global prosperity (including their own) and development in the Third World. In Richard Jolly's discussion of OECD policy-making in Chapter 9 this is made especially evident.

As befits a patron when he interacts with his clients, there is a certain sense of *noblesse oblige* in Northerners' approaches to the South. "More in sorrow than in anger" they must respond to the Southerners' unrealistic representations and explain to them how they have erred in their understanding. There is a certain amount of charade, pretence and hypocrisy in the North's apparent willingness to engage in (endless) further study of Southern proposals. In firm possession of truth (and power) already, they have no intention or need of discovering new truths, least of all from what to them is so unlikely a source. Negotiation and further study permit delay and distract attention from the "hidden agenda" for international decision-making which is negotiated in private somewhere else entirely. Northerners often genuinely believe that logical and factual errors abound in the details of Southern proposals, and that some of their proposals could therefore be prejudicial to development or inequitable in their distribution of benefits; but it would not and does not matter if they thought that their arguments were faultless. By now neither side believes what the other side says. The mutual credibility of ostensibly intellectual arguments in North-South debates has been severely impaired.

It is possible to conceive of a "leap" of perception, following which the world would be viewed quite differently and the impact of all global events upon developing countries (and vice versa) would acquire a new and much greater significance in Northern policy-making. There are sound arguments for Northern moves in this direction in the North's own interest (Brandt et al. 1980, Sewell 1979). One frequently senses that such a leap has already occurred among many members of the North's younger generation. Glimpses of such "vision" can sometimes be seen in the speeches of Northern statesmen. And it clearly is the hope that such a new vision might be jointly arrived at, and pushed downward upon traditional bureaucrats, that motivated the Brandt Commission's recommendation of a summit conference on North-South issues. Once arrived at, such a new "frame of reference" could give new meaning to the much-abused term of "interdependence".

Issue by issue, bargains which take the needs of developing coun-

9

tries into greater account might then be struck. Northern policy "success" would then no longer necessarily consist of "talking issues to death" and simply stalling any change. Theorizing about international economic phenomena, whether market or non-market, would then place the implications of events for the economic development of Southern countries at centre stage. But even in such circumstances, the underlying economic paradigms could conceivably still inhibit progress.

(iii) *Reasonable Objectives for Economic Theory*
Clearly, to seek to improve the underlying economic theory of the functioning of the world economy is not to seek to influence next month's policy formation. The object is a much longer-term one. If the pessimists are right, the next several years will be ones of global economic turmoil during which progress in North-South dialogue will be tortuously slow and most unlikely to produce significant change. When serious dialogue resumes and the potential for change again surfaces, it would be well to have the theoretical ground more adequately prepared than it has been in the past.

One must not, of course, exaggerate the potential power of abstract ideas or underlying "frames of reference". If *realpolitik* rules and if the major powers are content to leave the world more or less as it is, no amount of independent academic scribbling, no matter how brilliant, will have the slightest effect upon policy or upon change. Even those most sanguine about the ultimate power of theory and models expect their effects to be apparent only in the longer run (by which time the economists concerned, following Keynes' dicta, will be either defunct or dead). Ideas and frameworks change only very slowly. Moreover, action does not always wait upon theory. Dramatic changes in actual events sometimes produce "shock" effects in the world of ideas. More frequently, however, changing facts have little short-term effect upon basic models; and it is only a longer-term shift in the accepted model which will generate new behaviour. In the meantime, theory is usually called upon merely to rationalize or legitimize the way in which the world at present works.

Economic theory in major areas of North-South dispute

The developing countries have placed particular emphasis in recent years upon reform in the *institutions* of the international economy —

the IMF, the World Bank, the GATT, etc. — and upon the effects of the "institution" of the transnational corporation in private markets. It can be argued that institutions do not matter much in the face of the realities of political power and/or the forces of the market. To some degree, these are empirical questions, and are amenable to research exploration, through both historical and cross-sectional comparisons. Why are they not given more attention by Western scholars, particularly those in the Anglo-Saxon tradition? At least in part it is probably again because of the relative insignificance of non-market institutions in their theoretical apparatus, in which that of the competitive market is *assumed* to be dominant while all others are assumed to be either constant or irrelevant or both. (There has emerged a literature on the economics of hierarchies and internal organization, as opposed to the economics of markets; but, while it has attracted some of the most powerful minds in the field, it still remains on the periphery of the economics discipline.) On the face of it, the North nevertheless regards the preservation of the present institutional machinery as of very great importance, since it seems to have "dug in" to defend it.

Indeed, it is quite remarkable that such estimates as there are of the efficiency or redistributional costs to the North of accepting NIEO proposals are all very small. Some NIEO measures seem likely to involve "positive-sum games" and thus to be positively beneficial to the North. Estimates of the gains or losses to the North from implementing the South's proposals are obviously subject to some dispute; but since even the largest estimates of possible costs to the North are extremely modest in the aggregate, the North's opposition must be based on other considerations. It has been suggested, particularly by Alfred Maizels in Chapter 10, that Northern intransigence is not based upon the likely short-term costs of the programme, but stems instead from the fear of *losing control* of the entire system. (From this perception flows the implication that too much progress on the part of the South in the assumption of control over the global institutions could result in the North opting out of them in favour of its own independent ones.) Such considerations cannot be easily incorporated into traditional approaches to economic issues. Nor can the alternative prospect of catastrophic "negative sum" outcomes from continuing international disagreements. But they clearly merit more detailed investigation.

It is easier to assess the contribution of underlying economic theories by relating them to specific issues of North-South dispute; and

11

this is how we now proceed. In this procedure, however, there is no intended implication that the broader issues for theory are less important than those which can be related to narrower policy questions.

In some instances, traditional theory has run into serious problems in terms either of the validity of its assumptions or its predictive power or both. In the case of the theory of international trade, for example, policy-makers receive little guidance therefrom as to which industries they should encourage in order to benefit from the advantages of dynamic comparative advantage; and even less assistance in their attempts to assess the distribution as between the various interested parties of the overall gains from international trade. Both rich countries and poor are hampered by the inadequacies of existing underlying trade theory as they grapple with one another and among themselves over industrial promotion and location decisions, relations with transnational corporations, and state trading bargains. In the meantime, traditional free-trade incantations are ritually repeated while policy proceeds independently through a series of *ad hoc* measures, specific to individual industries and firms, in directions unrelated to any known theoretical map.

In other cases, it seems that theoretical approaches are not in such a state of disarray, but that differences in the importance assigned to different objectives and differences as to the "stylized facts" of particular cases nevertheless lead to quite different policy prescriptions. Thus, existing macro-models in the eclectic centre of the profession can be employed to generate more or less similar predictions, provided that there is agreement as to the likely size of various key coefficients within the models. The "structuralist" alternative to traditional IMF analyses of balance of payments adjustment mechanisms rests upon alternative assumptions as to the elasticities of import and export demand and supply, the behaviour of capital markets, the functioning of the price mechanism (in factor as well as product markets) and the like. Differences in policy recommendations also stem from different degrees of emphasis upon the equity of distributional impacts. In such cases, there is greater hope that the sustained application of economic logic and the collection of more relevant empirical material might gradually achieve agreed changes in policy approaches; or so it would appear from the recent efforts of the Group of Twenty-four to contribute independent high-quality professional assessment (in the form of the Dell report) to the discussion of IMF policies. This is not to suggest that underlying preconceptions as to the appropriate role of the state, the performance of markets, etc.

12

will not continue to lurk behind macro-policy recommendations or that disagreement as to the role of IMF conditionality as against automaticity will disappear. It is only to make the point that there is hope in this area that the ground within which agreement can be reached may be wider than in some other areas in which the underlying theory is inadequate.

In the case of international commodity markets, too, there may be found some rays of hope for achieving a theoretical consensus, though there is none at present. Traditional Northern analyses have been based upon the competitive market paradigm, with modifications considered on a case-by-case basis where "market imperfections" are particularly blatant. Southern approaches might be characterized as starting from a bargaining or conflict model, more akin to bilateral monopoly or oligopoly/oligopsony theories, with cases of competitive markets treated as the "imperfect" aberrations from the general case. Both approaches are clearly correct; each in their own "favourite" cases. There is emerging a relevant literature within the Western tradition which, in effect, is at least partially legitimizing the Southern approach by applying the tools of empirical analysis to particular commodity markets. These theoretical "bits and pieces" have not yet percolated through either to introductory Western textbooks or to Western economic policy-makers; but their volume may already be great enough to permit the thought that the dominant paradigm may yet shift to that of the South, particularly as the debate shifts away from price stabilization issues and towards those of marketing, processing, and distribution. At a minimum, it will in future be more difficult to generalize on the basis of the traditional models.

There is a screening and sifting process by which economic analysis of different kinds, reaching different conclusions, moves from those who first prepare it to those who actually employ it in decision-making. Traditions and interests combine to produce biases in the analyses prepared and employed by different institutions and different governments. Authors know what their employers need to hear, and, if they do not provide them with what they require, their results may in any case be weeded out. Nor is the professional distribution system neutral. There are instances of quite mediocre papers, sometimes even addressing matters that are not at the centre of dispute, receiving enormous professional and popular attention while others of superior quality languish utterly neglected. One would require the skills of a sociologist of knowledge to uncover all of the reasons for these phenomena. In part, professionals are as guilty as others of seeking out and disseminating the results which their personal backgrounds and experiences lead them to welcome; the footnote references employed by rival protagonists in academic disputes are often disconcertingly lacking in common items. Academics are also inclined to feature the unexpected and counter-intuitive results which, in the case of North-South issues, are more likely to discredit Southern than Northern initiatives. (There are, after all, not many Northern ones, since the North does not seek changes.) There is no doubt that negotiators make extremely selective use of the available knowledge, and some are not above the commissioning of "independent" studies which "prove" what is required. There is in such cases only a fine line between the provision of information and propaganda.

The following discussion considers, in turn, some of the major elements in the underlying economic theory of (i) international trade in manufactures, (ii) international primary commodity trade, and (iii) international monetary issues. The discussion of manufactured goods trade draws especially on my own Chapter 3 and Chapters 4-6 by Stein Rossen, Frances Stewart, and Ricardo Ffrench-Davis. That on primary commodity trade flows from John Cuddy's Chapter 2 and, to some extent, Alfred Maizel's Chapter 10. For the discussion on international monetary issues further argument can be found in Chapters 7 and 8 by John Williamson, and Edmar Bacha and Carlos Diaz-Alejandro, respectively.

(i) *International trade in manufactures*

International trade theory has been so refined and qualified in the specialized academic literature of the subject as to have been left with very few real-world conclusions. But in the world of Northern trade policy-makers the tenets of static comparative advantage theory and its factor endowment basis remain the touchstone for all debate. "Free trade" is the standard by which performance is to be measured; and poor countries are to specialize in exports which are intensive in the use of unskilled labour and such natural resources as they may possess. Southern demands in the North-South dialogue in the sphere of trade in processed and manufactured products are generally couched in terms of the same simple paradigm of liberal trading that Northern spokesmen and the GATT secretariat espouse; above all else, the South seeks reduced Northern protectionism against Southern manufactures. But the South's own performance often fails to square with these same principles of theory.

Southern pressure for reduced protectionism is clearly not part of a call for structural reform in the international economy but simply a call for the translation of the conclusions of orthodox trade theory into Northern freer trading practice. Whether the specific targeting of the share of global manufacturing which is to be located in the developing countries by the year 2000, as found in the Lima programme of UNIDO, is any more than the necessary consequence of the fairly orthodox policies which the South is pressing must be a matter of judgement; but it could easily be interpreted to a considerable degree in such moderate terms, rather than, as it often is, as a call for massive market intervention. As will be seen below, there are nevertheless theoretical grounds for the developing countries' adoption of more aggressive industrialization strategies within their own economies than free trading principles would imply.

Fully consistent with their use of the orthodox liberal paradigm in the sphere of international trade is the South's position on the regulation of restrictive business practices at the international level. Principles and rules, or codes, governing anti-competitive practices, including those engaged in within transnational corporations, are very much in the spirit of the GATT paradigm even if they are being developed primarily under UNCTAD auspices. Provisions of this kind were found in the original Havana charter for the International Trade Organization, and many Northern policy-makers have genuinely regretted that they were not included in the GATT.

In the real world of international trading practice, many of the assumptions strictly required for the policy conclusion that "free trade is best" are, of course, violated. Among the factors that must vitiate the conclusions of the simple trade models are: scale economies, market concentration (oligopoly and oligopsony), intra-firm trade, significant transport costs, state trading, product differentiation and non-price competition, unequal technological capacities, costs of adjustment as between different productive structures, imperfect information, and existing tariff and non-tariff barriers. Among the profoundly important structural features of the international trade of the 1970s and the 1980s is the dominant and rising role of transnational corporate activity therein. The developing countries have been particularly concerned with the implications for them of this particular institution for global management, within what are ostensibly "free markets"; their pressure for "liberal" trading is directed no less at the North's transnational corporations than at Northern governments.

The construction of development-oriented industrial policy, whether in rich countries or in poor, proves to be extraordinarily difficult in such a "second"- or "third-best" world. Particularly troublesome have been the handling of "learning" effects. While it is relatively easy to identify the major "losers" in which a country is relatively inefficient, it is extremely difficult to determine those industries in which one may best *acquire* a future comparative advantage. How then is one to decide upon a rational and globally efficient allocation of the world's industry? The simple static Heckscher-Ohlin formulations based upon relative factor endowments simply do not carry one far enough. If productivity improves with experience, early-stage protection of apparently unsuitable industries or firms may in the longer run be sensible. If such learning is industry-specific it also would seem to call, other things being equal, for industry specialization rather than diversification in the industrial sector. The implications for trade policy, and for development impacts, of a theory which builds upon the assumption of industrial learning differ sharply from those of the "standard" model. Whereas the latter suggests that all developing countries with a labour surplus should specialize in labour-intensive industries, the former implies that, as experience and scientific and technical resources differ among countries, so does the capacity to "learn" through different kinds of industrialization; thus countries which are further along in their capacity to learn will benefit from different industrialization strategies, and their pursuit will probably open up even wider gaps in the short to medium term between them and less fortunate developing countries.

The more effective incorporation of scale economies — as well as learning effects — into the modelling of international trade will also significantly influence the theory's policy implications. Since the gains which can be realized through increasing returns to scale, where they exist at all, can be expected to dwarf those attributable in traditional theory to marginal reallocations of production and consumption, it follows that in many industries "big is beautiful". Scale economies may be found in information processing, financing, marketing and distribution, and research and development, as well as in production. From theories building heavily upon the fact of scale economies and learning effects one may derive the conclusion that trade should be "free" and conducted overwhelmingly by very large trading units, whether private or public.

Where comparative advantage is diffused or unclear, and information is imperfect, such underlying theory could imply that large size or specialization are what matters most. It may be preferable quickly to specialize in *something* rather than endlessly arguing the relative merits of alternative industries on the basis of benefit-cost calculations of dubious reliability. Technological characteristics may provide as good a set of "rules of thumb" for the selection of new industries as any other, e.g., "appropriateness" of products, potential for learning effects, availability of scale economies, etc. The truth of the matter is that, although such an approach may seem a counsel of despair and an invitation to planning approaches asserting that "anything goes", knowledge of the roots of future relative industrial efficiency remains remarkably scant. All of these considerations also have obvious relevance to schemes for South-South industrial cooperation and joint industrial planning.

These scale and learning effects are among the underlying theoretical explanations for the rise of transnational corporations and state trading in international exchange. The selective promotion of freer trade by Northern policy-makers has amounted, in substantial degree, to the encouragement of the growth and geographic interpenetration of Northern-based transnational corporations. Theory has lagged substantially behind practice in this realm. If the allocation of resources both within and across economies, the determination of patterns and prices in international trade, the burden of adjustment to recession or other global shocks, and other such major issues are to be substantially affected by the managerial decisions of large transnational firms rather than through the interplay of market forces, then more theory relevant to their decision-making processes is required. Attempts must be made to model the interactions between large transnational corporations and large (primarily Northern) national governments, and the implications of their behaviour and their bargains for smaller actors. For this purpose, it would seem fruitful to draw much more upon theories of industrial organization, managerial decision-making, and bargaining and game theory, rather than to attempt to patch up existing trade theories with altered assumptions as to factor mobility, factor-intensity characteristics, and the like. (Certainly the assumption of internationally immobile capital is, in any case, no longer tenable.)

It can be argued that the growing and interacting roles of large governments and large firms in international production and exchange can render much more plausible the eventual introduction of the international taxation systems, which, if properly constructed, could help to overcome some of the problems which transnational corporate activities now create. Transfer price manipulation and arguments over the disposition of total tax revenues could be eased by international tax regimes which should now increasingly be explored by fiscal theorists rather than just by tax accountants and lawyers, as the importance of these issues continues to mount.

A further issue arising for Southern trade policy-makers in the context of such amended theories of international trade is the future productivity of the strategy of "export-led" growth. If learning effects dominate in the industrial development process and in the determination of dynamic comparative advantage, then specialization for export either because of factor endowment advantages or because of scale economies may or may not be the optimal policy. In a world of slower Northern growth, greater numbers of developing countries coming onstream with industrial exports, transnational corporate control of much of world trade, and protectionism in those sectors in which transnationals are weakest, export-oriented industrialization in the South may either bog down in worsened terms of trade or achieve success only at the cost of increasing transnational corporate control of the Third World's national economies. For many developing countries, no less important than the terms of GATT bargains or Northern governments' trade policies will be those of the daily bargains to be struck with the foreign firms which produce or market their manufactured exports. For the purposes of understanding or influencing such bargains either with private actors or over the size and terms of quotas and marketing agreements to be negotiated with foreign governments, theoretical underpinnings remain slight indeed.

It would seem that "conventional" economic analysis is potentially much richer than the caricature of it generally presented in policy-makers' speeches to buttress free-trade anti-*dirigiste* positions, but that a "revised theory" is not yet sufficiently integrated to form a coherent whole which would be immediately relevant to North-South trade negotiations or policy formation. Moreover, the potential richness derives much less from theoretical refinements of the neoclassical model of international trade than from the insights offered by resort to industrial organization, learning, and bargaining theories. The integration of these theories with international trade theories, incorporating the many qualifications necessary for realism, is perhaps the most formidable task now on the agenda for future research.

18

(ii) *International primary commodity trade*

Primary commodities have been at the centre of attention in the NIEO negotiations since they began. One of the cornerstones of the NIEO was to be the Integrated Programme for Commodities, including the Common Fund, the former a giant stabilization and development programme for 18 commodities of special export interest to the developing countries, the latter the central financing institution which would tie the various commodity programmes together into a cross-subsidizing package.

Although price stabilization objectives were by no means universally regarded as the most important ones in the commodity sphere, negotiations came to centre upon them. A substantial body of neoclassical literature existed, demonstrating that, under particular assumptions, price stabilization would be good for the world as a whole but harmful, in terms of income effects, either to producers as a group or consumers as a group, depending upon whether price instability originated from shocks on the demand or the supply side. An additional strand of this literature demonstrated, again with carefully stipulated assumptions, that the stabilization of prices would stabilize or destabilize the incomes of the producers as a group, depending upon whether price instability originated from the demand or the supply side. The complexity of the issues is illustrated by the fact that, under the assumptions typically employed, the same circumstances that would achieve income increases for the producers as a group through price stabilization would destabilize their total incomes. Considerable attention was paid in Western capitals to the studies which demonstrated these results, and Northern governmental positions on the Integrated Programme, the Common Fund, and individual proposed international commodity agreements appeared to have been influenced by them. The ambiguities and trade-offs implied in these results created occasions for endless debate, and called into question the wisdom of the South's pressures for price stabilization on the ground that it frequently might not serve the South's own interests.

Unfortunately, the "results" of the theorizing described above are misleading. They are extremely sensitive to the detailed assumptions of the underlying models, as has been carefully demonstrated by further theoretical analysis which has continued within the neoclassical tradition from which the original models sprung. The range and implausibility of the assumptions required to arrive at conclusions which have been cited in innumerable Northern policy position papers are truly breathtaking. They include particular shapes of both

19

demand and supply schedules (they must both be linear); particular kinds of demand and supply shocks (they must be additive to the relevant schedules and not multiplicative); instantaneous reactions of supply and demand to price alterations; and complete stabilization of prices at a fixed price equal to the mean of the prices which would have prevailed in the absence of intervention. Modification of any of these assumptions so as to approximate reality more closely, or simply to test sensitivity, results in the collapse of the widely cited conclusions. These qualifying theoretical contributions have not yet significantly penetrated the Northern policy-makers' perceptions. Needless to say, none of these theoretical contributions questions the underlying model of free and competitive markets, which is required to permit the employment of supply and demand schedules as representations of reality in the first place. Nor do they address the *real* problem of "market failure" created when speculation and panic buying and selling in commodity markets generate periodic "crises", which must somehow be "managed".

Whether these debates over the effects of price stabilization were of much real significance to the commodity negotiations is, in any case, an open question. Certainly negotiators pick and choose among available sources to find "objective" sources of support for positions which they have already arrived at on totally different grounds whenever they can do so. In at least one instance (the copper negotiations), one set of Northern negotiators discarded the (public) results of the very econometric modelling exercise they had earlier insisted upon, when it failed to yield the expected, and "required", conclusions.

At real issue are typically such matters as the interests of producing and trading firms of different nationalities, strategic interests in supplies, concerns over the eventual effects upon the level of prices and the size and allocation of export quotas. In the longer run, ownership and control of processing, marketing and distribution are clearly much more important concerns than price stability. Northern policy-makers' direction of attention to the theoretical issues surrounding the effects of price stabilization deflected it away from these more fundamental questions. They were and are able to do this at least in part because knowledge of the actual structural characteristics of commodity markets is still so scant. Most commodity markets are characterized by a high degree of concentration on both the buyers' and the sellers' sides. Many are highly segmented in their structure, with intra-firm trade within transnational corporations, state-to-state trading arrangements, long-term contracts among private and state transactors, and "free" residual markets all operating at the same time. Sufficient proportions of world commodity trade are "managed" either by private or by state actors as to make nonsensical the exclusive resort to models that imply only atomistic and competitive participants on free and unfettered markets — the models that still dominate Northern policy-makers' presentations and apparent perceptions.

Southern approaches to commodity questions are based less on detailed knowledge as to the actual functioning of markets than on a fairly crude perception that prices are set on the basis of bargaining and conflict rather than through neutral and impersonal free and competitive markets. Their paradigm is quite different from that which Northern spokesmen employ, and in this instance it is often at least as accurate. Both Northern and Southern spokesmen can point to specific instances in which their own simplified "model" best describes reality. While it may be difficult to agree on which is more generally accurate, it should by now be possible to build a middle-ground theoretical structure which eclectically takes both market and bargaining approaches into account.

To adopt, even in part, a bargaining model of the determination of international commodity prices is to resurrect the controversial issue of the developing countries' terms of trade and the possibility of indexing their export prices to the prices of their imports. Even in the citadels of market orthodoxy, domestic agricultural prices are determined by political processes as well as purely market forces. Such possibilities can be realized regardless of the make-up of the developing countries' export or import bills; but, because of the Prebisch-Singer theoretical backing from which the proposals originally sprang they have been couched in terms of linking the prices of primary product exports to those of manufactured goods imports. That such "stabilization" of certain relative prices (actually, the proposals were intended merely to set a floor to real commodity prices) can have allocative effects is beyond dispute. What exactly they would be depends upon a host of assumptions as to governmental policies and private responses. Conventional economic theory has been employed to demolish the proposals for the international indexation of primary commodity prices on the grounds of their inefficiency effects. Possible social "inefficiency" has never been, however, a significant element in the striking of bargains over domestic distributional questions. The basic irrelevance of such considerations in bargaining situations is demonstrated by the present general interest in quite

21

similar proposals for the stabilization of the price of petroleum. Once again, conventional economic theory still has little contribution to make to the analysis of bargaining.

What is sorely lacking from the underlying theory of North-South trade either in primary commodities or in manufactures is an adequate explanation (or justification, which is a much more controversial matter) of the distribution of the gains therefrom. The Prebisch-Singer analysis attempted to analyse it through the concept of the terms of trade, and thereby addressed the effects of changes through time. Emmanuel has based his analysis upon the international immobility of labour and focusses upon labour's entitlement to equal remuneration for equal productivity, regardless of its location.

Neither have proven persuasive or rigorous enough to have been incorporated into the central "core" of trade theory, although both have clearly an enormous intuitive appeal. Here is another rich area for theoretical exploration. In this connection, the incorporation of transnational corporate activity into the relevant models, as was suggested above, would seem to call for new concepts of the terms of trade which are based upon national "retained value" from exports rather than conventionally measured prices for export products.

(iii) *International Monetary Issues*
Those engaged in current North-South debates over international monetary issues, while they may argue over the finer points, all understand and employ basically the same underlying economic models of macro-economics and balance of payments adjustment. There is neither a paradigmatic clash, as in the case of commodity market analysis, nor rampant confusion and massive dissonance as between theory and practice, as in the case of trade in manufactures. What is at issue is, fundamentally, the distribution of financial power and control; and the objectives of development policies. At a more prosaic level, there are also often differences as to the "stylized facts".

Developing countries, as poor countries faced with current account deficits that are not always of their own making, seek monetary reforms that will ease their balance of payments financing difficulties. They seek greater symmetry of balance of payments adjustment responsibilities, so that countries in surplus and reserve currency countries share short- and medium-term adjustment costs. They seek greater resort to SDRs as the source of international liquidity expansion and greater shares of their distribution, so as to acquire a higher proportion of the seigniorage from "money creation" which at present accrues to reserve currency countries and gold producers and holders. Not surprisingly, they also seek greater influence and voting power within the International Monetary Fund so as to push the reforms which they favour.

The most important immediate source of North-South disagreement is over the terms of developing countries' access to international finance, and specifically to the resources of the IMF. (Since commercial banks may await the IMF "seal of approval" much more than IMF lending may be at stake.) The "conditionality" question involves disagreement as to (i) the appropriateness of the present degree of conditionality in IMF lending, and (ii) the terms of the conditions which it typically imposes.

In the first instance, the developing countries view the IMF's approach as excessively rigid and excessively influenced by the assumption that balance of payments difficulties are the product of domestic monetary mismanagement; where balance of payments deficits are the product of external shock rather than of domestic mismanagement, there should be a *prima facie* case, they sensibly argue, for unconditional balance of payments support. This is particularly evident if these external shocks are temporary ones — and not necessarily those of only a year or two's duration; but, even if they are permanent and long-run adjustment is necessary, IMF support should be assumed to be readily available to assist the process. The principles governing such low-conditionality balance of payments support have already been recognized in the IMF's compensatory financing and oil facilities. At present, the availability of low-conditionality financing is inadequate; the result is resort to private banks and/or inappropriate deflation.

Secondly, when the IMF makes recommendations on domestic policies, it has frequently carried with it the biases described above as implicit in conventional neoclassical theory — it over-emphasizes market measures and downplays the influences (real or potential) of such institutions as the state or the transnational corporation; and it does not concern itself overly with the distributional implications of alternative macroeconomic policies. Nor does it consider, though this is a matter of wider global concern, the need to maintain longer-run development momentum in the poorer countries. It has therefore tended to apply a fairly standard set of policy prescriptions to *all* countries: reduced government expenditures (particularly cuts in social service spending, food subsidies, and wages, since these are both more visible and more politically acceptable to many governments

23

than cuts in defence budgets or civil service salaries), higher tax rates, domestic credit ceilings and higher interest rates, liberalization of exchange controls and devaluation, all of these to be applied relatively quickly in a "shock" rather than a "gradualist" manner.

This uniform deflationary package may be quite appropriate to some circumstances. It is most unlikely to be appropriate for all. A powerful and theoretically rigorous "structuralist" critique of the IMF's standard package has now been constructed in Latin America. It addresses the impact upon income distribution, total aggregate demand, inflation, and the balance of payments, and concludes, on the basis of assumptions which are not implausible (notably as to elasticities of demand and supply, pricing systems, wage-setting mechanisms, and capital flows) that the IMF package can be counterproductive in the short- to medium-run; and that the longer run in which events might improve is not guaranteed ever to materialize. Similar criticisms of IMF rigidity can be heard in Asia and Africa as well. The critique of the IMF package is not a critique of adjustment policies themselves (although in popular discussions these matters are sometimes confused), but of the particular package which typifies the IMF approach. Recent revisions of IMF guidelines suggest that at least its Executive Board, if not yet all of its operative personnel, now recognizes that the nature and timing of adjustment programmes must be tailored more closely to fit the circumstances of particular countries. The elaboration of "better" policy packages is still in its infancy and deserves further study.

The distinction between finance for purposes of balance of payments adjustment and for development is not always an easy one to draw. It is particularly difficult when recessions are longer-lasting and when there are major shocks, such as oil price increases, which require long-term adjustment. In such circumstances, balance of payments finance for the purpose of "riding out" longer storms or for easing the process of structural (supply) adjustment begins to merge into development finance. When the IMF offers longer-term adjustment loans and the World Bank offers structural adjustment loans, both are employed for essentially the same purposes.

In recent years there has been a sharp increase in the relative importance to the developing countries of private money and capital markets. Commercial banks operating in the Euro-currency markets have channelled very large sums to the more credit-worthy of the developing countries. The criteria for the allocation of these resources, as derived from standard portfolio theory and applied by unregulated private banks, deviate significantly from those which the internationl community might apply if it controlled the disposition of those resources; among other reasons, this is because the objective function in that community's decision-making does not, as does the private portfolio theory, ignore income distribution. Thus, in particular, practically all of the money lent by the Euromarket to the Third World has gone to the middle-income countries, and none to the poorer ones. As in all asset markets, changes in investors' expectations, which themselves are vulnerable to the herd instinct, can generate significant "lurches" into and out of particular kinds of lending, with the result that the amount and composition of commercial bank lending to particular developing countries is inherently unstable. At the same time, the concentration of these banks' lending on so few countries, and the sheer magnitude of the resources so channelled, raise concern for the stability of the whole international financial system should one of the "select" countries actually be unable to repay its debts, causing some of the banks themselves to risk failure. Here, accepted Western macroeconomic theory, combined with theory of the developmental effects of income distribution, indicates strongly that the view held by many in the international financial community, that the private capital markets have handled and can continue to handle such recycling well, may be seriously in error. Deserving of further theoretical exploration are the implications of regulation (in order to reduce the moral hazard problem) as against *laissez-faire* policies in international financial markets for the interests of the developing countries.

None of the above monetary disputes will cause great anxiety to orthodox theoreticians or to the policy-makers who negotiate these North-South issues. The discussions proceed on the basis of models which are broadly intelligible and acceptable to both sides. Disagreements are either the result of differences in judgement as to the "stylized facts", in which case they can presumably be resolved by further detailed research and analysis, or the product of underlying conflict over the international distribution of income and power. In the latter case, again, a theory of bargaining is required for a more complete understanding as to what is actually taking place.

Recommendations for further research and activity

The growing interdependence of national markets for goods, services, technology, capital, and some kinds of labour have increasingly limited the capacity for national sovereign governments to pursue fully independent policies. Just as the various actors within nations are interdependent and governments have been created for the purpose of assigning and enforcing rules which are in the social interest, so at the international level there is a growing need for a global manager to "rein in" independent national actors, including governments, on the world stage. (And just as, at the national level, governments are pulled and hauled in their policy formation by special interests of divergent power, so it would also undoubtedly be the case for any global authority.) "International economics" must be replaced by "global economics" in theoretical analysis. Ultimately we are likely to acquire more effective global government, which can then employ it. The transnational corporations and, to a much lesser extent, the international trade union secretariats are already conducting their activities on a world basis — with effects that are still quite imperfectly understood. It is ironic that while governmental activities have steadily grown at the national level in the mixed economies of the post Second World War period, and this growth has generally been considered to be legitimate, there has been no corresponding expansion of governmental activity at the world level, where unrestrained market forces and the law of the jungle still seem to be considered more legitimate than any threats on the part of global authorities to national sovereignties. Economic theorists and modellers must surely now begin to apply their general tools of analysis to the problems of the one "closed economy" which, until interplanetary travel opens up, still remains: that of the entire world. Only when national policymakers begin to employ such comprehensive "frames of reference" in their own decision-making can one expect to find international issue resolution on the basis of higher global interests. Existing attempts to model the entire world — in the UN, the World Bank, the OECD, the ILO, and the Bariloche Foundation, for instance — are still fairly crude, mechanical, and apolitical.

In the shorter run, there is a great need to improve theoretical understanding of the individual economic issues in North-South disputes, and to raise the quality of the economic analysis which is brought to bear upon them. In this paper, attention has been particularly focused on the shortcomings of the economic models implicitly or explicitly employed by Northern negotiators. It would be ridiculous to attempt to argue that only the North's negotiators have been biased in their use of available theory or that their implicit models are more rigid or crude than those of others. Nor, despite their obvious efforts to propagate their views, are Northern policy-makers dispro-portionately guilty of conscious or unconscious propagandizing. On the contrary, it is the very "liberalism" and catholicity of Western traditions that permits us to criticize the way in which its policy-makers employ their knowledge. But there can be no doubt that in the North-South arena, the North has far, far more than its share of the "good lawyers". Academia, the media, and government spokes-men have together so swamped the advocates for the South with their (too crude) arguments that they have created a mood within which Southern arguments are almost automatically ascribed to "un-reason", or "bad economics"; they are assumed to be "illegitimate" almost as soon as they are made, and it becomes Northern sport to see who can first firmly prove them so. The transnationalization of knowledge through postgraduate training, scholarly journals, and the press furthers the legitimization of Northern positions, and ex-tends even into the academic institutions and governmental offices of the South. Intellectual hegemony may be no less powerful, enduring, and ultimately defensive of privilege than any other kind.

Much of the economic analysis employed in the backing of parti-cular cases *is* complex. The North's supply of academic and other professional talent for the purpose of making its case, or at least legi-timizing it, is enormous — far superior to that available to the policy-makers of the South. Whether the most important case-makers are lawyers or economists, the South is clearly *always* at a major disad-vantage. As one participant in our seminar vividly put it, it is often possible for Northern policy-makers to denigrate well-informed and cogent Southern arguments with statements which amount to saying, "Hocus-pocus; mumbo-jumbo; therefore you are wrong". If what we are observing is essentially a bargaining relationship rather than a search for truth, there must be a presumption that, to the extent that arguments play any role at all as against the realities of power, the outcomes will be consistently skewed against the least prepared. Both the search for balance in knowledge, and sympathy for the under-dog, should generate far more professional effort to pick holes in Northern rather than Southern arguments, even if it does not pay as well.

Such questioning of orthodox paradigms as there has been tends to appear either in specialized professional journals, which do not re-ceive wide circulation, or in the "radical" literature, which is not read by policy-makers. The markets for intellectual fare — to use neoclassical terminology — are highly segmented ones; and, as usual,

27

such market imperfections generate social inefficiency. It is not possible to prescribe an alternative core model to which all "right-thinking" analysts should immediately shift, for it does not exist. But it is important to address the deficiencies in the current dominant models, note their disproportionate influence, and call for attempts at reform. One must attempt somehow to integrate more effectively the better and more relevant "bits and pieces" on the frontier or the periphery of economic theory into the relevant "core" approaches. One must, in short, do what one can to reduce the dogmatism of the intellectually untravelled.

In areas where there is disagreement as to the "stylized facts" there is an obvious need for the careful assembly of more detailed information. This may be a particularly fruitful area for collaborative North-South research, particularly if research partners are not selected for their known bias towards "desired" outcomes. As has been seen, this may yield especially high returns in the sphere of commodity market functioning and balance of payments adjustment in different types of developing countries.

Among the specific areas relevant to the North-South and NIEO disputes which seem particularly deserving of more theoretical or modelling attention are the following:

(i)   analyses of bargaining — among individual governments, blocs of governments, large firms, interest groups within and across national boundaries, and combinations of all of them; the world has become at least as much a "bargaining society" as a "market economy";

(ii) analyses of the distribution of the gains from international trade, as between nations, firms, and component groups and classes within nations;

(iii) analyses of international trade which incorporate elements of industrial organization theory, the theory of managerial decision-making, and bargaining theories, so as better to capture the roles played by transnational corporations, the major national governments, and the interactions among them;

(iv) analyses of the functioning of imperfect and segmented world primary commodity markets; and commodity processing, marketing and distribution activities;

(v)   analyses of dynamic comparative advantage which incorporate such elements as industrial learning effects at different stages of development, scale economies, and the growth of firms, and may enable developing countries more effectively to "pick the winners", and to improve their national or regional industrial planning;

(vi)   analyses of the size and distribution of the costs of adjustment to both macro-economic and relative price "shocks" in global or developing countries' economic systems;

(vii) analyses of the unfettered and regulated functioning of international financial markets and their development implications;

(viii) analyses of transnational corporate decision-making and behaviour in general, and in different specific industries and circumstances, and their development implications;

(ix)   analyses which relate the questions of power and control of institutions to the traditional ones of income maximization and risk aversion, considering the possibility of trade-offs and the role of time;

(x)   analyses of the political economy of governmental decision-making in matters of international economic policy.

In each of these areas there is an obvious parallel need for empirical research to enrich and enlighten the theorizing process.

Progress will be achieved, if at all, only through a gradual process of experimentation, exchange of ideas, intellectual agglomeration effects, and continuous testing and revision. Bridge-building across intellectual and experiential chasms seems especially likely to prove productive. Among the ideas that arose from our group's deliberations on these matters were the following:

(i)   it is especially fruitful to conduct discussions between those who are very well-versed in the details of relevant theory in a particular issue area and those who were themselves directly involved in policy formation and negotiation (in the Refsnes seminar, this was most effective in the discussion of commodity issues);

(ii)   when introducing fresh concepts or approaches, even when persuaded that older ones should be replaced, one should seek to translate them into the more familiar terminology so as to facilitate communication, understanding, and ultimately persuasion;

(iii) collaborative research between economists who begin from different paradigms, and preferably come from North and South, should be encouraged or even commissioned, in areas like international trade theory or commodity market functioning where "breakthroughs" are most required;

(iv) consideration should be given to the sponsorship of a series of detailed surveys of "the state of the art" of underlying theory in each of the major North-South issue areas so as to bring "laggards" up to date and encourage the pushing back of the theoretical or empirical frontier in the weakest segments of knowledge; if one author were up to the task, an across-the-board booklength survey might do as well or even better; in the meantime, perhaps effort should be devoted to the collection of already published works into a book of relevant readings on these subjects.

The task of building new theory is not an easy one. Nor have attempts to prescribe approaches to the development of knowledge ever been very successful. But dissatisfaction with what one has can be a powerful motivator; at present, it is still much more widespread in the South than in the North. This volume has not been designed, to use an old phrase, "to afflict the comfortable and comfort the afflicted" in the North-South dialogue. Rather, it is intended to prod academic thought and effort into particular directions. The world now badly needs more economists and others working to improve existing theories of the functioning of the global economy, and to disseminate more effectively the full range of such knowledge as already exists.

References

Brandt, W. et al. 1980. *North-South: A Programme for Survival* Pan and MIT.

Dell, S. (United Nations) 1979. *The Balance of Payments Adjustment Process in Developing Countries: A Report to the Group of Twenty-Four* (UNDP/UNCTAD Project INT/75/015, 1979).

Hansen, R.D. 1979. "Can the North-South Impasse be Overcome?" Overseas Development Council, Development Paper 27. November, 1979.

Keynes, J.M. 1936. *The General Theory of Employment, Interest and Money.* Harcourt, Brace and Co., New York.

Sewell, J.W. 1979. "Can the North Prosper Without Growth and Progress in the South?" In Martin M. McLaughlin et al. *The United States and World Development, Agenda 1979.* Praeger.

Part I
International Trade Theory
and
North-South Negotiations

Chapter 2

Theory and Practice in NIEO Negotiations on Commodities

*J.D.A. Cuddy**

The negotiations of a new international economic order (NIEO) take as their basis UNGA resolutions 3201 and 3202 (S-VI) on the "Declaration" and the "programme of Action" on the establishment of an NIEO. Although these resolutions contain an almost endless catalogue of propositions and exhortations on commodity issues, the "reservations" of the Western industrial countries ("Group B" in UNCTAD parlance) were almost equally numerous, with the result that the attention of the international community has been focussed mainly on two major issues in commodity policy: indexation and stabilization. This paper will examine these two issues in the context of what might be called "practical orthodoxy", i.e., the explicit or mental models used by Western economic policy-makers (particularly in the USA, UK, Japan and FRG).[1]

Indexation

The notion of indexation, in regard to the NIEO and international commodity policy, relates to the linkage of the prices of raw materials exported by developing countries, and the manufactured goods which these countries import. The intellectual justification given by proponents of indexation lay in the Prebisch-Singer tradition of terms-of-trade immiserization of the "Periphery": workers in the Periphery are made worse off by technical progress there if the Periphery's income elasticity of demand for the Centre's export goods is sufficiently high and the (absolute value of the) price elasticity of the Periphery's import demand sufficiently low (Bacha 1978). From this sprang the self-evident proposition that if the resulting balance-of-payments problems which required employment levels in the Periphery to decline could be avoided by fiat, all would be well. Hence

* The views expressed in this paper are the author's alone, and should not be taken as an expression of the views of the organizations with which he is affiliated.

the idea of linking the prices of Periphery exports to those of Periphery imports.

"Accepted western economic theories" were soon brought to bear to demonstrate the futility of pursuing this goal unless either the consumers themselves agreed to do so (e.g., via multilateral contracts, by means of which, somewhat incredibly, the chickens would themselves help to pluck their own feathers) or the primary goods in question were strongly cartelizable (however, with the exception of a few minor — but admittedly strategic — minerals, petroleum seems to be the only commodity of importance to the developing countries for which this is true). The standard neoclassical theory equally indicated the inefficiency of an indexation mechanism (could one be found) in the allocation of resources, since it would freeze relative prices in a manner that took no account of subsequent movements in comparative advantages.

Moreover, even if technically feasible, a doubtful enough proposition in itself, the success of an indexation prescription was predicated upon assumptions about the short-run and long-run price elasticities of Centre demand for the Periphery's export goods, assumptions which, with a few exceptions, seemed at variance with empirical evidence. Nevertheless, the mere suggestion of such a scheme spawned a violent reaction on the part of the Western economic policy-makers (WEPs, for short), which is the subject of this paper.[2] This reaction was couched almost exclusively in terms of a rejection of "dirigisme" or interference in "free markets", although such other arguments as that indexation would ineluctably lead to increased global inflation (a proposition based in part on the assumption that indexation would work only in the upwards, and never in the opposite, direction), did surface from time to time. That such a response by the WEPs to the notion of indexation was disingenuous, at the very least, seemed evident enough to most observers of the negotiations; for example, it was never for a moment admitted by the Northern negotiators that much in their domestic agricultural policies bore a striking resemblance to the basic notion of "parity" which lay behind the concept of indexation. Yet the very tenacity with which the WEPs stuck to their phraseology suggested strongly that, as Keynes had warned, they must be prisoners of an economic model whose relevance to the real world was, to put it mildly, rather doubtful. In that ideal, static, neoclassical, textbook model lurked the assumptions (among others) of perfect competition, riskless certainty, atomistic producers and consumers, full domestic factor mobility (but international factor immobility), complete freedom of entry, total lack of externalities, full international consumer sovereignty, freely available production technology, and optimal pre-existing income distribution; it has been the object of severe criticism for its lack of realism for some time now (Helleiner 1979). Yet appeal (stated or implicit) to its results was largely the basis for WEP statements in regard to indexation during negotiations dealing with that subject.

Of course, there was more to WEP pronouncements on indexation than met the ear. As anyone who has been one knows, WEPs must respond eclectically to the various "pressure groups", the intrusion of whose positions is an essential part of Western policy-making. Indeed, in many circumstances, the views of these pressure groups are taken to constitute national objectives; and this was particularly true in regard to indexation, since the declarations of the pressure groups concerned — the various associations of manufacturers who feared the hideous prospect of gratuitously increased raw material prices — could, with hardly any effort of projection on the part of WEPs transfixed with concern over inflation, be assumed to represent the views also of that essential portion of the electorate, the "consumers". Thus, it would seem, the appeal by the "practically orthodox" WEPs to economic models had much less to do with their response to the indexation proposal than did their concern with an immediate, short-run domestic policy problem — the dramatic rise of inflation characteristic of the period in which the indexation proposal was put forward and which (ironically) constituted the very *raison d'etre* of the proposal itself. For the idea of indexation was born, not of a sudden flash of enlightenment in the Third World in which the truth of Prebisch's terms-of-trade immiserization theory was at once evident to all, but rather of the startling decline in the purchasing power of a unit of Third World exports over imports of rapidly inflating First World manufactures, exemplified by President Nyerere's impassioned evocation of the increase in the tonnage of coffee or cocoa or groundnuts exports needed for the purchase of a single imported tractor.

Of course, the WEPs responded also to this kind of proposition, by trotting out captive academics who repeated the standard litany, already chanted in the fifties, regarding the impossibility of saying that Third World (net barter) terms of trade tended over time to deteriorate, because of quality changes, different base periods and the like. Much was made by the WEPs of the fact that a panel of experts, convened (ironically) by UNCTAD, had been unable to discover clear-cut proof of such a tendency during their cursory examination of a very limited sample of data (Brown 1980, pp. 162, 315); they conveniently ignored, however, evidence assembled by the World Bank and by UNCTAD (Cuddy 1976a) that, whatever the long-term tendency, certainly over the period from the end of the Korean War, the net barter terms of trade of primary commodities vis-à-vis manufactures *had* significantly deteriorated.

With perhaps more force, however, some WEPs pressed the point that the interference in markets upon which depended the success of any "direct" indexation scheme of the sort discussed above, was quite unnecessary, since the implicit objective of transferring resources to the South to preserve (or even improve) the earning power of their exports could also be achieved, without intervention, via what was called "indirect" indexation (Cuddy 1976b). Such a scheme would merely "compensate" (from some central fund) countries which would have received higher prices under direct indexation for their unrealized gains. Indeed, it was emphasized, this kind of scheme, modified to be based upon a partial insurance principle, entailing a revolving fund and restitutions when prices rose above the reference level, is precisely the basis of the STABEX scheme, which forms a cornerstone in the Lomé convention between the EEC and the associated ACP countries. As, however, the reference level for the STABEX scheme does not in any way take account of those import prices which are the essence of the "direct" indexation proposal, this line of argumentation seemed slightly beside the point, to put it politely.[3]

All of this discussion became moot, however, when the commodity price boom of 1973—75 relieved the pressure (in regard to manufactured imports) for most Third World countries. This demonstrated once again the slender "relevance of accepted Western economic theories to the negotiations of a new international economic order" (the announced title of the conference for which this paper was prepared), but for the perhaps awkward reason that practical short-run concerns of governments (First or Third World) always take precedence over issues of longer-term or broader relevance. It is doubtful whether improvements in the underlying theory would have any impact on the attitude of WEPs to indexation proposals in the future. The same might not, perhaps, be true of the attitude of WEPs to proposals regarding the stabilization of commodity markets, an apparently positive-sum game. To the study of this issue this paper now turns.

Stabilization

The issue of commodity market stabilization has been much more extensively investigated than has indexation, and there is a voluminous literature on the subject, most of which concentrates on the stabilization of commodity prices.[4] Since this, too, has been a major focus of international negotiations on commodities, it will be the primary concern of this part of the paper; but first it may be useful to dispose of a red herring frequently thrown into the negotiations.

It is clear enough that if price is completely stabilized but output fluctuates, income will fluctuate. Since in reality price will never be completely stabilized, the appropriate question is whether or not, in the face of partial price stabilization, the remaining fluctuations in income are greater or less than before. In the negotiations the WEPs have instead posed the issue starkly as an alternative between price stabilization and earnings (income) stabilization, in an apparent attempt to deflect the discussion away from UNCTAD's Integrated Programme for Commodities towards their own preference for reliance on what is known as "compensatory financing" schemes, of which the facility of the same name at the IMF provides one example.[5] Partly, the desire to focus on compensatory finance derives from what some call the "hidden agenda" of the negotiations, namely the suspicion (in some cases, certainty) on the part of the WEPs that the demand by developing countries for price *stabilization* is really a stalking horse for attempts at price *raising*. Partly, it is related to the "anti-dirigiste" attitude discussed above. Seldom does it seem to derive from a serious analysis of the comparative costs and benefits involved. Moreover, it can at least be argued that compensatory finance schemes do not attack the root problems in the commodity markets because they are merely *ex post facto* devices designed to palliate the effect of losses of export earnings already incurred precisely because of the instability of commodity markets. In fact, they can be an expensive palliative: it has been shown (Cuddy 1978b) that it is possible both to stabilize commodity prices *and* to stabilize export receipts by using an IPC-like mechanism with residual compensatory financing for the same financial expenditure as is required merely to support a full-fledged compensatory financing system. For this reason, this issue will not be pursued more than incidentally in what follows.

Conventional economic analysis has evaluated the price stabilization issue from two perspectives: (a) theoretical; (b) empirical. On the theoretical side, orthodoxy has flowed from the Waugh-Oi-Mas-

37

sell tradition (Massell 1969, Oi 1961, Waugh 1944) of examination of supply and/or demand shifts in simple (usually linear) models, neither explicitly incorporating private stockholding behaviour, nor taking any account of the institutional framework within which real-world commodity markets function. Although the theoretical analyses of Turnovsky (1974, 1978) and others (e.g., Just *et al.* 1978, Newbery 1976) have advanced beyond these extremely simple models (although still not explicitly modelling private stockholding behaviour), what has in this paper been called "practical orthodoxy" has not evolved very far from the earlier approach.

A case in point is the study by McNicol (1978), at the time a consultant to the US Treasury Department and subsequently heavily involved in US commodity policy, both in Washington and as a delegate to multitudinous Geneva commodity conferences. Another example, much quoted by WEP delegations to commodity conferences and very influential in those Western capitals seriously examining the issues, is the World Bank study by Brook, Grilli, and Waelbroeck (World Bank 1977).[6] Both the Bank and the McNicol studies adhere strictly to the Massell-type structure, which requires, to quote the Bank study, the assumptions of:

"(a) linear and negatively sloped demand curve, linear and positively sloped supply curve;
  (b) instantaneous reaction of supply and demand to price changes;
  (c) parallel shifts of demand and supply curves over the two periods (additive stochastic disturbances); and
  (d) price stabilisation at the mean of the prices that would have prevailed in the absence of market price stabilisation." (p. 6)

The essential theoretical conclusion of these studies is that "the integration of the income and welfare effects of price stabilisation shows how important is the knowledge of the prevalent source of commodity price instability... (D)eveloping countries as a group can be seen to be clear gainers from price stabilisation ... in those commodities whose prices fluctuate mostly as a consequence of supply disturbances and where developing countries are net exporters of the commodity in question (which is the normal case)" (World Bank, 1977, p. 17).

Quite aside from the host of unrealistic assumptions which underly all models in this Massell tradition (to which I turn later), it is important to note that these influential studies ignore previous theoretical advances made even within their own tradition. In particular, the assumption of additive stochastic disturbances is quite inappropriate for the supply function, in which yield fluctuations will naturally be proportional to acreage. Turnovsky (1978) examined this case and concluded that the distribution of the benefits of stabilization *"does not depend upon the source of price instability,* as it does in the additive case" (p. 127, italics in the original). Thus, the whole focus of the Bank and McNicol studies on the identification of the unstable "culprit" is totally misplaced when a simple adjustment towards reality is made in the models. Yet WEPs — by and large speaking for the consuming community — have continued to argue that price stabilization for agricultural commodities will be "bad" for consumers because "if market price instability originates mostly from supply shifts, producers (exporters) will gain from price stabilisation ... and consumers (importers) will lose" (World Bank, 1977, p. ii) and "the prevalent source of commodity price instability ... (is) supply for most agricultural products" (*ibid.,* p. 24).

Another important problem with these studies, again a deficiency remedied by further theoretical work within the same tradition, is that they assume costless stocking operations which immediately and permanently stabilize the price at that value which equates demand to supply. But, as Wright (1979) has pointed out, the stabilized price "cannot be maintained indefinitely ... (because) the commodity stock will follow a random walk as long as that price is maintained. But the stabilising capability of storage is asymmetrical ... (since) the ability to contain price rises in the face of repeated shortfalls is limited by the size of the stock ... and the price is not completely stabilised in the long run" (Wright 1979, p. 1016). Moreover, no stocking scheme ever discussed in the NIEO negotiations has aimed at maintaining a fixed price; rather, it is proposed that prices be contained within a band around a long-term equilibrium level. Furthermore, Nguyen (1980) has shown in the context of the linearly additive Massell-type model, that such *partial* price stabilization can *completely* stabilize commodity export earnings even when market instability is predominantly supply induced. Thus, another step towards reality in theoretical formulation makes the results of the Bank-McNicol studies appear even less relevant to the negotiations on the NIEO.

More generally, there are severe defects in the neoclassical model that underlies these studies and forms the basis for WEP analysis of stabilization proposals in the NIEO negotiations. Perhaps the major defect from the present paper's perspective is that the neat results of optimal resource allocation and welfare gains from trade depend upon the neoclassical theorist's abstraction from institutional reality, in particular the assumption of a perfect market whose atomistic participants maximize their utilities and where factors are rewarded at the rate of their marginal productivity, resulting in Pareto-optimal efficiency of resource allocation. Such assumptions are clearly at serious variance with the characteristics of actual markets. Several of the participants of this conference have already analysed the "imperfections" of existing markets (e.g., Helleiner 1979, Diaz-Alejandro 1976, Vaitsos 1974) and Smith has recently surveyed "failures" in commodity markets (Smith 1978). What emerges from these and other surveys of the actual markets in which commodity trade takes place is essentially that they bear very little relation to the idealized market of the neoclassical theorists; oligopoly, state intervention, intra-firm trade, unequally powerful participants, scale economies, concentration of technological knowledge, tariff and non-tariff trade barriers — all these elements and more compound to vitiate the results of standard neoclassical theory.

Consider the commodity markets for a moment. It has been argued (e.g., Fama 1970) that speculative markets generate and process information efficiently, in the sense that prices therein adjust quickly and correctly to new information. Some WEPs have extended this thesis to cover the commodity markets, at least those for which future exchanges exist. However, there is considerable evidence that such an extension to commodity markets of the Fama hypothesis, even if true for other markets (and Naidu 1980, has recently presented evidence that it is not, for the foreign exchange markets) is invalid (see e.g., Houthakker 1961, Gray 1961, Stevenson & Bear 1970, and Praetz 1975). Other WEPs have argued that if instability in commodity markets were such a bad thing, and stocking was a way to correct the markets' errors, private stockholding should do the job; but authors from Keynes (1938) onward have demonstrated that there is room for public stocking because private stockholders tend towards excessive risk aversion, which cannot be transferred and optimally pooled in "risk markets" because these do not exist, at least in regard to commodities. Thus, as Smith points out, "government intervention in storage is desirable ... because whatever imperfections result from the absence of explicit risk markets are likely to generate ... costly distortions in very risky activities such as commodity storage" (1978, p. 172).

Moreover, even if commodity markets did operate efficiently in the sense defined by Fama, there are obviously other factors which would justify stabilizing governmental intervention. I have discussed the case for such intervention elsewhere (Cuddy 1979b), but it may be useful here to note three such additional factors: (i) the apparent existence of a "ratchet" effect of commodity price increases on domestic inflation and the ensuing deflationary policy response (Cooper & Lawrence 1975, Kaldor 1976); (ii) the uncertainty generated by unstable markets, which leads to incorrect forecasts of future prices and thus to over- or under-production (or investment in production); and (iii) the negative effects on developing-country growth of unstable commodity export earnings, disputed by many (e.g., MacBean 1966) but recently demonstrated convincingly by Lancieri (1978, 1979).

These points are, of course, additional to the "imperfections" caused by the massive concentrations of economic power in the hands of transnational or state trading corporations in many commodity markets. As Kostecki (1977) has pointed out, "the most significant portion of the developed countries' state trading is trade in food grains and some raw materials"; he also notes that his data "seem to confirm ... that the 'liberally minded' United States counts among the most important state traders in absolute terms (perhaps even outstripping the USSR on Western markets)" (pp. 19—20). But even this important state trading of the Western industrial countries (accounting for perhaps 10—15 percent of trade, according to Kostecki (1977, p. 20)), is not so all-pervasive as in developing countries: state trading plays an important role in the trading of "a wide range of goods in some South American economies and in a majority of countries in Black Africa", as well as in such important Asian countries as India, Pakistan, Sri Lanka, Indonesia and Iraq (Kostecki 1977, p. 19); nor need the role of state trading in COMECON countries be forgotten.

As to the concentration of power in the hands of transnationals, perhaps only a few examples will suffice: in the cotton industry, fifteen large corporations handle about 90 percent of the world's cotton trade, eight American, five Japanese, and two European; needless to say, their weight in determining prices on the supposedly "efficient" New York Cotton Exchange is dominant (Clairmonte & Cavanaugh 1978). In addition to this, about one-third of world cotton exports is handled by governments or public corporations (UNCTAD 1977). In the aluminium industry, over two-thirds of bauxite mining and alumina refining are held by a mere half-dozen major transnationals, and a further one-fifth of bauxite mining capacity is held by governments in developing countries (UNCTAD 1980). Similarly, over two-thirds of the banana trade in most western industrial countries is accounted for by but three transnationals (UNCTAD 1974).

The message about neoclassical theoretical structures is clear; moreover, it is, of course, not unknown to WEPs. What is perhaps particularly unpleasant about the appeal by WEPs to this patently unrealistic theoretical apparatus in the NIEO negotiations on commodities is that the very same WEPs abandon the apparatus when it comes to sectors in which their own economies' interests are at stake.[7] Thus, too much "free marketeering" is not a good thing: while there must be no intervention in the jute or copper markets, intervention (of a perhaps somewhat different form) is a necessity in the textiles, steel, automobile, shipbuilding and electronics industries, to avoid "disruptive" change in these sectors.

Conclusions

What does the analysis sketched above have to say about the "relevance of accepted western economic theories to the negotiations of a new international economic order"? In the first place, perhaps, it warns — and this will be news to no one but the most naive — that these theories are of very slender relevance indeed to WEPs, who will use or discard them as fits their purposes in the negotiations. Thus, for example, the basic US attitude towards international commodity agreements, when all the rhetoric is stripped away, changes depending on whether the US is primarily a producer or primarily a consumer, of the commodity in question. It also varies with the strength of the various lobbies whose vested interests are at stake. Consider the case of wheat, for which international commodity agreements of various forms have been in place since 1947. Although the US[8] has agreed to the principle of a stocking mechanism for wheat (of which, of course, it is the world's major producer), it has insisted strongly that the mechanism be based on a "quantity trigger" rather than the "price trigger", on which it has insisted with equal force in agreements for commodities (like tin, cocoa, and rubber) of which it is a major consumer. Surely the reason could not be that the flow of data on quantities is sufficiently slow that the mammoth American transnational grain companies would, in a period of high prices, stand to make handsome profits for a much longer period of time under the quantity trigger approach than under the price trigger approach!

The second conclusion I would draw from the analysis made in this

42

paper is that the neoclassical theory itself is so riddled with patently unrealistic assumptions basic to the theoretical conclusions that, regardless of whether or not WEPs will pay it any heed in the near term (when the negotiations on the NIEO are being carried out), the intellectual integrity of the economics profession demands that wholesale revisions be made to the theory. This is not to suggest that much useful work in this direction has not already been carried out; but it has not been usefully integrated into the mainstream of economic analysis. For example, the theory of imperfect competition has been with us for a long time; yet very little of it has worked its way into commonly applied economic models. In the context of commodities, some interesting attempts to do so have been started by Epps (1975) and Jaksch (1979), but these have not yet progressed very far. Such revisions amount to (substantial, it is true) tinkering with the basic neoclassical structure; they still ignore, however, the important, if presently ill-developed, thrust of the "unequal exchange" school (Emmanuel 1972), which is clearly groping for an intellectual structure that is more relevant to the aspirations of the vast bulk of the world's population than is a theory that takes existing income distribution as acceptable and tries to find Pareto-optimal adjustments to it. It seems to me that it is in these directions that the economics profession must now channel its efforts if it is to avoid being consigned to history's dustbin of obsolescence.

Notes

1 As Rothstein (1979) has pointed out "the spectrum of views within Group B was well-known: the United States, West Germany, Japan, and the United Kingdom on the right; the Nordics and the Dutch on the left; and the rest scattered about ... The Germans ... were the strongest defenders of the virtues of the market ... The Japanese were properly inscrutable and seemed content to hide behind the American Treasury." (pp 123—5)
2 For a thorough discussion of the US position, which largely dominated, by a former US Treasury official, see Vastine 1977.
3 For a fuller discussion of the STABEX scheme, see Cuddy (1979a). See also note 5 below.
4 See Brown (1975) for a useful summary of the "traditional" literature. Cuddy (1978a) and Hallwood (1979) survey more recent literature.
5 Stripped to their essentials such schemes would provide loans to a country should its foreign exchange earnings from exports fall short of a pre-determined target level and would require repayment of the loan when export earnings exceed this target. The difference between such schemes and the "indirect indexation" schemes dis-

cussed above is that the latter have a price-based trigger, whereas the former have a value-based trigger. The STABEX scheme is actually a hybrid, since the compensation trigger is based on value, but the restitution trigger is based on price.

6 Grilli at the time was a member of the Bank's Commodities Division; subsequently he moved to an important position with the influential Italian Confederation of Industries, and has recently been appointed Director of the Bank's Commodities Division.

7 One particularly apposite example of this Janus-faced approach occurred during negotiations in Geneva when the WEPs, having successfully demanded that the UNCTAD secretariat commission one of the WEPs' own "captive" consultancy firms to do an expensive study of the effects of partial price stabilization of the copper market (rather than use the opportunity-costless but suspect resources of the UNCTAD secretariat), then rejected out-of-hand the results of the carefully conducted study, apparently since it seemed to suggest that such stabilization might be a good thing for the global community and not nearly so demanding of (investment) resources as the WEPs had been wont to insist would necessarily be the case.

8 Prior to the Reagan administration's "Block-ing" approach.

References

Bacha, E. 1978. "An Interpretation of Unequal Exchange from Prebisch-Singer to Emmanuel", *Journal of Development Economics,* December, 1978.

Brown, C. 1975. *Primary Commodity Control.* Kuala Lumpur: Oxford U.P.

Brown, C. 1980. *The Political and Social Economy of Commodity Control.* London: Macmillan.

Clairmonte, F. & Cavanaugh, J. 1978. "Cotton Trading: Futures for the Few", *Development Forum,* July, 1978.

Cooper, R. & Lawrence, R. 1975. "The 1972—75 Commodity Boom", *Brookings Papers on Economic Acitivity,* No. 3.

Cuddy, J. 1976a. *International Price Indexation.* Lexington, Mass: Lexington Books.

Cuddy, J. 1976b. "Preservation of the purchasing power of developing countries' exports" (UNCTAD document TD/184/Supp. 2).

Cuddy, J. 1978a. "Commodity price stabilisation: its effects on producers and consumers", *Resources Policy,* March, 1978.

Cuddy, J. 1978b. "The Common Fund and Earnings Stabilisation", *Journal of World Trade Law,* March/April, 1978.

Cuddy, J. 1979a. "Compensatory Financing in the North-South Dialogue", *Journal of World Trade Law,* January/February, 1979.

Cuddy, J. 1979b. "The Case for an Integrated Programme for Commodities", *Resources Policy,* March, 1979.

Diaz-Alejandro, C. 1976. "International Markets for Exhaustible Resources: Less Developed Countries and Transnational Corporations", Discussion Paper No. 256, Yale University, December, 1976.

Emmanuel, A. 1972. *Unequal Exchange: A Study of the Imperialism of Trade.* New York: Monthly Review Press.

Epps, M. 1975. "A Simulation of the World Coffee Economy", in Labys, W. (ed.) *Quantitative Models of Commodity Markets.* Cambridge, Mass.: Ballinger Pub. Co.

Fama, E. 1970. "Efficient Capital Markets: A Review of Theory and Empirical Work", *Journal of Finance.*

Gray, R. 1961. "The Search for a Risk Premium", *Journal of Political Economy,* June, 1961.

Hallwood, P. 1979. *Stabilisation of International Commodity Markets.* Greenwich, Conn.: J.A.I. Press.

Helleiner, G. 1979. "World Market Imperfections and the Developing Countries", in Cline, W. (ed.) *Policy Alternatives for a New International Economic Order.* New York: Praeger Publishers.

Houthakker, H. 1961. "Systematic and Random Elements in Short-term Price Movements", *American Economic Review,* May, 1961.

Jaksch, H. 1979. "Oligopolistic Behaviour on the World Cocoa Market", mimeo.

Just, R. et al. 1978. "The Distribution of Welfare Gains from Price Stabilization", *Journal of International Economics,* November, 1978.

Kaldor, N. 1976. "Inflation and Recession in the World Economy", *Economic Journal,* December, 1976.

Keynes, J. 1938. "The Policy of Government Storage of Foodstuffs and Raw Materials", *Economic Journal,* September, 1938.

Kostecki, M. 1977. "State Trading in the Industrialised Countries and the Developing Countries", *Les cahiers du C.E.T.A.I.,* April, 1977.

Lancieri, E. 1978. "Export Instability and Economic Development: A Reappraisal", *Banca Nazionale del Lavoro Quarterly Review,* June, 1978.

Lancieri, E. 1979. "Instability of Agricultural Exports: World Markets, Developing and Developed Countries", *Banca Nazionale del Lavoro Quarterly Review,* September, 1979.

MacBean, A. 1966. *Export Instability and Economic Development.* London: George Allen and Unwin Ltd.

Massell, B. 1969. "Price Stabilization and Welfare", *Quarterly Journal of Economics,* May, 1969.

McNicol, D.L. 1978. *Commodity Agreements and Price Stabilisation.* Lexington, Mass.: Lexington Books.

Naidu, G. 1980. "How the Filter Lets a Profit Through", *Euromoney,* June, 1980.

Newbery, D. 1976. "Price Stabilisation with Risky Production", *Economic Series Working Papers,* No. 69, Stanford University, May 1976.

Nguyen, D. 1980. "Partial Price Stabilisation and Export Earning Instability", *Oxford Economic Papers,* March 1980.

Oi, W. 1961. "The Desirability of Price Instability under Perfect Competition", *Econometrica,* January, 1961.

Praetz, P. 1975. "Testing the Efficient Markets Theory on the Sydney Wool Futures Exchange", *Australian Economic Papers,* December, 1975.

Rothstein, R. 1979. *Global Bargaining.* Princeton: Princeton University Press.

Smith, G. 1978. "Commodity Instability and Market Failure: A Survey of Issues", in Adams, G. & Klein, S. (eds.) *Stabilising World Commodity Markets.* Lexington, Mass.: Lexington Books.

Stevenson, R. & Bear, R. 1970. "Commodity Futures: Trends or Random Walks", *Journal of Finance,* March, 1970.

Turnovsky, S. 1974. "Price expectations and the welfare gains from price stabilisation", *American Journal of Agricultural Economics,* November, 1974.

Turnovsky, S. 1978. "The Distribution of Welfare Gains from Price Stabilisation: A Survey of Some Theoretical Issues", in Adams, F.G. & Klein, S. (eds.) *Stabilising World Commodity Markets.* Lexington, Mass.: Lexington Books.

UNCTAD 1974. Document TD/B/C.1/162, December, 1974.

UNCTAD 1977. Document TD/B/C.4/157, February, 1977.

UNCTAD 1980. Unpublished working paper, Commodities Division.

Vaitsos, C. 1974. *Intercountry Income Distribution and Transnational Enterprises.* Oxford: Clarendon Press.

Vastine, J. 1977. "United States International Commodity Policy", *Law and Policy in International Business,* No. 2, 1977.

Waugh, F. 1944. "Does the Consumer Benefit from Price Instability?", *Quarterly Journal of Economics,* August, 1944.

World Bank 1977. "Commodity Price Stabilisation and the Developing Countries: The Problem of Choice", *Staff Working Paper,* No. 262, July, 1977.

Wright, B. 1979. "The Effects of Ideal Production Stabilisation: A Welfare Analysis under Rational Behaviour", *Journal of Political Economy,* October, 1979.

Chapter 3

International Trade Theory and Northern Protectionism against Southern Manufactures

Gerald K. Helleiner

Introduction

International trade theory has a lot to be humble about. Beyond the general principle of comparative advantage, which can be applied to persons and corporations as well as to nations, it now has very little firm support on which to hang understanding or policy. It has never had a satisfactory explanation of the distribution between trading partners of the total gains from trade, contenting itself with Paretian questions as to whether they are each better off with trade than without it.

In recent years, not only have the simplified models of international trade typically employed in the classroom been called increasingly into question even by academics for their restrictive assumptions (see, however, Jones on "two-ness", 1979), but governmental policies also seem to be less related to their normative conclusions. At the same time, vigorous activity on the frontier of trade literature — theoretical refinements, empirical testing, etc. — has left it in a state in which it would be difficult for trade theorists now to agree as to what exactly current "orthodoxy" is.

In the most general terms, on the matter of international trade in manufactured products, "orthodox" theory seems to be on the side of the South. For many years Northern advice on Southern trade policy generally promoted outward-oriented and "orthodox" free trade approaches. It was for Southern theorists, spokesmen and policy-makers to find fault with the implications of open-ness and the pursuit of short-term comparative advantage; import substitution and the protectionism it usually required were usually denounced by Northern trade theorists on grounds of traditional theory, or patronisingly "explained" in terms of nationalistic preferences for smoking chimneys. Now that Southern manufacturing industry has attained the capacity to compete effectively in particular sectors upon global markets, it is in the North that there is more hedging on total commitment to traditional comparative advantage approaches.

The generalized debate between advocates of "free trade" and "protectionism" *is* one in which all are tempted to join from time to time. Particularly when there appear risks of protectionist "sea-changes" in the overall course of international trading policy most of us still take up liberal positions. But this general professional preference for "reasonably open" economies is far removed from the detailed concerns and prescriptions relating on a case-by-case basis to individual industries and sectors. On these, traditional theory is disconcertingly unhelpful. Those who purport to fall back on traditional "theory" to back their own "knee-jerk" reactions to specific cases and frequently almost fetishist liberal policy recommendations are typically either not in touch with recent literature or have managed so to compartmentalize their thinking that the new knowledge does not intrude too severely into the paradigm with which they have long been most comfortable. Understanding international trade in manufactures now requires a highly eclectic theoretical approach.

Traditional theory and reality

Among the major real-world difficulties for traditional simple models and the resulting "free-trade" remedies are:

(i)   market imperfections and distortions; where factor and product market prices are, for a wide variety of reasons, unreliable guides to social benefits and costs, all things are possible (Bhagwati 1971, Diaz-Alejandro 1975);

(ii) risk, uncertainty, imperfect and/or asymmetric information (Helpman & Razin 1978, Pomery 1979);

(iii) the costs of adjustment from one pattern of resource allocation to another and the need to trade long-term gains against short-term costs at an agreed rate of discount (Baldwin & Mutti 1973);

(iv) the still unknown dynamics and developmental effects (including "learning") of alternative patterns of allocation and change (Chenery 1961);

(v)   the detailed income distributional effects of alternative policies.

There are also new complexities, for policy purposes, in the definition of the maximand. It has been usual in trade theory to consider the objective of nations as the maximization of per capita (or sometimes total) national income. But is this tenable as a starting point in the

48

North today? *If* national objectives can be defined at all, they are likely to include other dimensions which are no less important than income levels. In particular, it is probably necessary to add to national objective functions today:

(i)   stability and reduced uncertainty of national and individuals' income;

(ii)   equitable national distribution of income; and perhaps

(iii)   improved quality of life — length and quality of labour force participation (work week, sabbaticals, age of retirement, "participation" in decision-making, security, etc.).

It is thus possible now to conceive of change — of whatever kind but especially if very rapid — as "disruptive", and therefore bad, even if it eventually leads to higher levels of income. Corden (1974) has described this as a "conservative welfare function". Unexpected large "shocks" can generally be assumed to be "worse" than repeated small or anticipated changes. (I believe this to be a matter of much more general relevance. Conventional tools are ill-equipped to assist us in the analysis of risk and uncertainty except in Bayesian terms. The only modern theorist — to my knowledge — who has grappled with the prospect of "shock" uncertainties and discontinuities of the kind the world now faces is Shackle (1955), with his concepts of "focus-gain" and "focus-loss". Perhaps his almost forgotten tool-box should be resurrected for the purposes of analysing "catastrophes", "systemic breakdown", and the like.)

Higher levels of income can also be rejected if they are associated with worsened income distribution. On the other hand, if suitable changes in working conditions, income distribution, etc. are achieved, it may be possible to make nations "better off" without any reallocations whatsoever.

In the sphere of positive and descriptive international economics, it is known *(not* in order of importance) that:

(i)   significant proportions of world trade take place on an intra-industry basis, i.e., they involve two-way trade within the same industrial classification (Giersch 1979);

(ii)   significant proportions of world trade also take place on an intra-firm basis, i.e., the buyer and the seller are branches of the same firm (Helleiner 1981);

(iii)   trade patterns can be explained by technology gaps, scale economies, trade barriers, transport costs, and other such variables at least as effectively as by traditional factor endowment ones; indeed traditional theory falls apart when the number of goods and factors expands or scale economies abound (Ethier 1979, Stern 1975);

(iv) global markets are frequently quite imperfect in the sense that market concentration, non-price competition, and product differentiation abound, and "the law of one price" is rarely to be found (Helleiner 1979, Isard 1977);

(v) the static welfare gains from abolition of tariffs and trade barriers — as measured by Harberger's little triangles — are invariably relatively small (Corden 1975);

(vi) non-tariff barriers to international trade — both governmental and private (restrictive business practices) — are of increasing relative importance as tariff barriers diminish (Sampson 1980);

(vii) the adjustment costs associated with altered international trading patterns are dwarfed by those resulting from technical change, demand shifts, and the business cycle (OECD 1980);

(viii) the structure of trade barriers imposed by particular countries can be understood at least as well (probably better) as the product of pressures from internal interest groups as in terms of "national interest" (Baldwin 1980);

(ix) transport costs — assumed away in most trade models — are usually at least as important in the determination of trade patterns as governmental trade barriers; and there are substantial imperfections in shipping and freight markets (Finger & Yeats, 1976).

A further fact that is highly relevant to discussion of Northern protectionism and/or adjustment, and one that it is most important to convey effectively to Northern electorates is that the North enjoys a substantial surplus in manufactured goods trade with the South; more fundamentally, that trade ultimately must be in balance.

Developments in the understanding of North-South trade in manufactures

Particularly relevant to North-South issues in recent years has been the progress of theorizing and research in the areas of non-tariff trade barriers, adjustment and the political economy of trade policy.

(i) Economics of Trade Barriers

Until relatively recently the effects of trade barriers have been analysed primarily in terms of tariffs. The standard textbook partial equilibrium analysis also proceeds on the assumption of perfect competition in the relevant product market, and, frequently, assumes that the importing country is too small to affect the world price. Standard effective protection measurement also proceeds from these assumptions together with more. The analysis of trade preferences (GSP, Lomé Convention, etc.) is usually similarly conducted. (With minimal extra effort the small country assumption can be relaxed and so can that of perfect competition.)

For many purposes, such simplifying assumptions can be justified. It is no longer possible, however, to analyse trade barriers without explicitly taking quantitative restrictions and other non-tariff barriers into account. There has been considerable progress in the analysis of import quotas, demonstrating the non-equivalence of tariffs and quotas (McCulloch 1973, Takacs 1978), and quotas and voluntary export restraints (Murray & Walter 1978). There are now valid theoretical reasons for the expectation that developing countries will always prefer voluntary export restraints to import quotas. The measurement of the effects of non-tariff barriers has proven a very difficult matter, however, particularly so when there is market concentration and/or vertical integration in the importing industry. Such measures as there are tend to be fairly crude, and seek merely to calculate a tariff-equivalent by comparing world prices with domestic ones for roughly comparable products, in cases where physical limitations are imposed by governments. (The distribution of the gains from the GSP has not as yet been very satisfactorily analysed either.)

Nor, needless to say, have we very useful tools for the analysis of the bargaining between importing and exporting countries over the size of physical restraints on trade or, within countries, over licensing mechanisms. On the effects of such non-tariff barriers as national favouritism in government procurement, the requirement of particular standards, or "industrial policies" of various kinds, there are as yet very few pointers at all. Even murkier are the effects of *private* procurement practices, frequently nudged in a protectionist direction by anxious governments. These are undoubtedly influenced by ownership ties and other firm-to-firm relationships. Can anyone "explain", for instance, the enormous differences in the structure of French and British prices for particular consumer-goods (which generate such enthusiastic shopping expeditions) when both ostensibly receive the same protection from world markets?

Even when there exists agreement as to the possible utility of particular tools of economic analysis in this sphere, they can obviously be employed for various purposes to yield answers to different kinds of questions. The questions that are asked and the assumptions upon which the analysis proceeds can be crucial to the conclusions which "economic analysis" is said to reach.

A striking instance of the speed and efficacy with which a "conventional wisdom" can be disseminated when it accords with Northern preconceptions and interests was the economic analysis of the effects of the Tokyo Round upon developing countries. On the basis of very simplified and aggregative analysis, Baldwin and Murray (1977) generated the result that developing countries as a group would gain more from across-the-board MFN tariff reductions by the industrialized countries than they would lose therefrom as a result of lowered tariff preferences. This study rapidly became the most widely quoted paper in Northern discussions of these issues, acquiring almost the status of ideology — and seeming to offer a firm demonstration of the developing countries' unreason. But Baldwin and Murray did not really explore the incidence of such losses as there might be; nor did they allow for the inevitable exceptions to the across-the-board cuts or the likelihood that cuts would fall well short of the authorized maxima. In the event, the developing countries' assessments of their prospects in the Tokyo Round (collectively and individually) were more accurate than the widely cited assessment of these "technical" analysts. (None of these comments are meant to disparage the honesty or integrity of the research in question.)

(ii) Economics of Adjustment

Naive models in which reallocation occurs painlessly and smoothly are no longer taken seriously in the North-South (or any other) trade discussion. The economics (and politics) of adjustment to import competition is a relatively young field of writing and reflection. The basic methodology for the estimation of the present value of prospective gains and losses from alternative policies for individuals, regions, groups and nations is quite straightforward. What has been lacking is detailed empirical work, not relevant theory; so far it has been confined to only a few countries (Baldwin & Mutti 1973, Jenkins et al. 1978, Wolf 1979).

Disagreement remains as to the appropriate Northern governmental policy response to the certain prospect of future industry-specific pressures from Southern competitors. Should it:

(i) be minimal, allowing the market and private initiative to carry the major responsibility for adjustment in whatever ways are individually seen as privately most profitable, as the GATT Secretariat seems to recommend;

(ii) consist of measures to increase the adaptability and mobility of factors of production, particularly labour, to facilitate the "positive adjustment" which the OECD Secretariat promotes;

(iii) involve attempts to forecast those industries in which pressures will soon be registered, in the hope that "anticipatory" adjustment programmes and industrial strategy can be deployed in a more "planned" manner, as the Japanese have done and the UNCTAD Secretariat and others have recommended? (Wolf 1980).

In order to assess the relative efficacy of alternative governmental adjustment assistance programmes, trade theorists have less to contribute than fiscal economists and authorities on the functioning of labour markets. In any case, the great bulk of private firms' adjustment takes place without reference to governmental programmes; its analysis is probably best conducted by industrial organization specialists with knowledge of the theory and practice of mergers, competition, scale economies, the growth and decline of firms, etc.

(iii) *Political Economy of Trade Policy*
Only within the last decade have political science and the theory of public choice been significantly mobilized to shed light upon why governments do what they do in the area of trade policy (Baldwin 1980). Since international trade policies are determined by national governments, it is crucial to understand their decision-making processes, and not simply rely upon crude assumptions as to their "probable" views of "national" interest. In one recent analysis of the U.S. tariff structure, for example, among the most powerful influences on current practices proved to be "inertia", as represented by the Smoot-Hawley tariff structure of 1930 (Lavergne 1981).

Further areas for theorizing and empirical research

Still under-emphasized in writings on Northern trade barriers, adjustment, and trade politics, is the role of scale economies and thus the transnational corporation. The new pressures from developing countries upon particular industrial sectors of the North can be accommodated in different ways. Even the most liberal of Northern economists and policy-makers have been heard in recent years to remark on the "difficulties" of "too rapid" adjustment. Transnational manufacturing and trading companies have frequently been at the centre of the most rapid adjustment processes and of the discussions as to appropriate mechanisms of response.

In recent years there has been much Northern discussion of the "organization" or "management" of international trade in manufactures. The same governments that appear to be horror-stricken at the prospect of "interfering" with world markets for cocoa beans or copper are anxious to achieve "orderly" change and "smooth" adjustment, and to form international "management" bodies for textiles, shipbuilding, steel, and automobiles. Governmental interventions are considered *de rigeur* whenever the pace of change is deemed to be too rapid and thus to cause "market disruption"; they can, when necessary, be undertaken unilaterally at the national level and do not have to await international agreements. International rule-making in these sectors is in disarray, as the safeguard clause (article XIX) in the GATT is still essentially inoperative. (The failure to repair it was the great failure of the Tokyo Round.) At the same time the international Multifibre Arrangement, which was imperfectly renewed in 1981, has created general disillusion on the part of both importing and exporting countries as to the potential for mutually satisfactory management agreements. The organization of world industry and thus of international trade in manufactures is clearly a major area for continuing North-South dispute.

The most recent manifestation of this dispute was in the disastrous UNIDO conference in New Delhi in late 1979. The failure of this conference was, above all, the result of disagreement over the size (and composition) of Northern official industry-related development assistance. It also revealed fundamental disagreement, however, over the feasibility and desirability of transferring to the sphere of intergovernmental negotiation the allocative decisions in respect of world industry which it has been usual to leave to "the market". It is important to recognize, in considering the merits of the Northern and Southern cases, that the pure workings of "the market" have already been severely infringed upon by governmental trade barriers, and hierarchical (bureaucratic) decision-making and planning systems within the private sector. The polarized debate between advocates/

opponents of "global bureaucracy" and "free markets" seems to take little note of current realities. One would think that discussion of industrial redeployment, adjustment and trade should at least begin from a common perception of facts.

In one segment of manufactures trade, a particular form of industrial organization has so far not led to the same degree of North-South intergovernmental dispute. Where the trade has been "free" from governmental intervention and has instead been "managed" by transnational corporations (or by importers of inputs for domestic Northern manufacturing activity), they themselves have somewhat "smoothed" the redeployment of their own global resources. These firms are obviously not "surprised" by the consequences of their own investment, importing and production plans; they do not feel any "market disruption". To the extent that, as a result of their increased imports, employment in these firms' Northern operations is reduced, there may be intense dispute, however, between the labour movement and the producing firms, and attempts on the part of labour to involve government on its behalf. (Even in these cases, the interests of higher-skill workers may conflict with those of the lower-skill displaced workers, with the result that the labour movement is not itself unified in its pressure upon firms and governments.)

As I have argued elsewhere, governmental barriers against "disruptive" imports into the North are much more likely when they emanate from firms which are truly "foreign" than when they originate in subsidiaries or affiliates of firms within the importing country (Helleiner 1981). Thus, Northern governments will be led to twist the incentive structure facing developing countries so as to favour "free trade" in those developing country exports which are "managed" by their own Northern firms; Northern *governments* need only seek to "manage" that trade which is not already effectively managed by their own private citizens (unless the latter are perceived to be managing it in ways that are widely perceived to be contrary to the social interest). The trade "liberalization " that emerges from Northern political systems is highly selective in respect of both sectors and trading partners.

Much as one might prefer the workings of competitive and arms-length markets, with "self-denying ordinances" (Tumlir 1977) reining in interventionist governments, the real world seems instead to be offering two "management" models from which to choose:

(i) One can leave it all to the transnational corporations, with a minimum of governmental impediments to their global rationalization efforts; this will be particularly appealing in those sectors already largely dominated by transnational corporations. Where scale economies and other factors create substantial advantages for large, transnational corporations, there are likely to be pressures for the establishment of "national champions" of one's own, whether private or public, in individual Northern countries. Firms from particular countries may possess comparative advantages in particular types of activities (Dunning 1979).

(ii) One can seek to develop new sectoral-level intergovernmental agreements to monitor events and set certain ground-rules for national and international conduct; the Multifibres Arrangement is the principal prototype for such agreements at the multilateral level, but there are also precedents within the OECD in the shipbuilding and steel sectors. These arrangements are most likely where either there are few transnationals and arms-length transactions dominate international trade (textiles, footwear) or where the government is itself active in production (steel, shipbuilding, airlines).

Must "free" trade also perhaps be planned trade? If so, is smooth, orderly, and equitable change achieved best through the planning efforts of (enlightened?) private firms or through socially responsive governmental and intergovernmental planning? Which form of planning is more likely to come unstuck?

If, as seems likely, transnational corporations are to continue to play an important role in the development of North-South trade in manufactures, no less attention should be directed to abuses of their "managerial" powers than to those of governments. One needs no "political" analysis of transnational decision-making, as one does for governmental trade policy, but one does require increased theorizing and understanding of international business. In particular, it will be necessary to continue the efforts to monitor restrictive business practices (provisions for the regulation of which were contained in the 1947 Havana Charter but are not found in the GATT), and abuses of transfer pricing. The newly multilaterally agreed (April 1980) "equitable principles and rules for the control of restrictive business practices" address these problems, but how effective these new codes will be remains to be seen. Of particular concern is the code's ambiguity concerning intra-firm trade. In the section on undue restraints on competition — price fixing, market or customer allocation, quotas, refusals to deal, etc. — (section D.3) there is specific exemption for enterprises "dealing with each other in the context of an economic entity wherein they are under common control, including through ownership, or otherwise not able to act independently of each other"; in that on the abuse of a dominant position of market power (section D.4) — notably in respect of discriminatory pricing — there is no such exemption. The leeway left by these provisions for cartel-like activity in intra-firm trade in what are only guidelines to begin with is the product of conventional Western legal conceptions of the corporate entity; it finds no justification in the neoclassical economic theory which underlies national and international efforts to regulate restrictive business practices.

We seem to have been witnessing an inexorable shift at the global level to larger-scale manufacturing and trading entities, a process that has been underway for the past 150-odd years. Scale economies in information processing, marketing and distribution are likely to extend well beyond the scales, sometimes quite small, at which production cost curves flatten out or even turn back upwards; no doubt, the importance of economies of scale varies considerably from sector to sector. Within the OECD there seems to be reasonable confidence that geographic interpenetration on the part of its members' own large transnational firms, particularly if somewhat reined in by antitrust laws and/or foreign investment vetting systems, can generate mutually beneficial and socially desirable outcomes. Intra-OECD conflicts certainly can be found — over "industrial policies", particular non-tariff barriers, etc. — but so far there is still a degree of consensus in the North that the overall process is itself benign. "Liberalization" of trade within the North now really means offering encouragement to the process of transnationals' growth and increasing interpenetration. It is not clear that a similar interpenetration between North and South is at present possible or desired by the North.

The future of North-South manufactured goods trade should therefore be seen as a matter of industrial organization, investment planning, the structure and power of domestic Northern political pressure groups, and all of the influences underlying them. The policy questions of the coming years are those of the location of new industry, the incentives affecting it, and the decision-making processes that both create these incentives and plan the investments. On the face of it, international trade theorists have less to say on these matters than theorists of industrial organization (internalization of trade, scale economies, market concentration, location decisions, the growth of firms, etc.) and public choice (including political scientists).

Further North-South division?

As has been seen, there is an emerging Northern consensus that there is no need to bear the full costs of sharp readjustments in industries in which *all* the Northern countries are uncompetitive relative to the newly industrializing countries, particularly where the imports originate with unrelated parties. At the same time, there are major doubts within the South about the international distribution of the gains from trade which is effectively managed by Northern transnationals (particularly when their own capacity to rein in or even monitor it may be limited), and about the universal efficacy of liberalization policies. Hence, we have the prospect of a fragmented world trading system: the North, agreeing within the GATT, the OECD, various summit conferences and other fora of its own, to abide by a set of trading rules which it no longer offers to the rest of the world on a MFN basis; and the South, reluctant to play by the North's rules, seeking to expand industry and trade on its own terms.

The "fortress OECD" scenario is already visible in the overtly discriminatory Multifibre Arrangement, the failure to reach agreement with the South over the safeguard clause in the GATT (thereby leaving Northern countries to apply their own rules in their trade with the South), the disappearance of the MFN principle from the newly negotiated GATT codes on non-tariff barriers, and the restrictions of OECD codes on transnationals and other matters to activities within the OECD. Exceptions to this North-South "divide" take the form either of "special relationships" of a patron-client character, such as the Lomé Convention and other more traditional reflections of spheres of influence (buttressed in a world of floating key currencies by currency alignments), or. of "graduations" (cooptions?) into GATT or eventual (perhaps partial) OECD membership or both, in cases where more advanced developing countries accept the obligations of such membership.

A further emerging strand of Northern governmental policy in respect of competition from other OECD sources (particularly from Japan) is the encouragement of transnationals' investment in new productive facilities within the importing country; such encouragement is achieved, above all, by threats of barriers to continuing arms-length imports. Where foreign transnationals are already producing nationally there is governmental pressure to increase local value added and local sourcing; in the case of smaller countries, efforts are also undertaken to achieve "world product mandates" for the national subsidiaries. These "deals" between Northern governments and Northern transnational corporations further the process of interpenetration, and expansion of Northern interdependence, and blur the lines between private and public management and planning. "Industrial strategy" — public and private — becomes the determinant of future patterns of trade. Few developing countries have transnationals and/or capital enough to be able to play this investment *versus* trade barrier game; until they acquire the capacity to do so, the presumption is that their "disruptive" goods will be kept out by trade barriers. "Non-disruptive" goods imported from foreign subsidiaries will not face the same barriers.

On the one hand, then, there is emerging a "core" of increasingly interdependent industrialized countries within which more coordinated or even common trade, competition, and macro-management policies will be inevitable. The distinction between domestic and international policies within the North seems likely to become harder and harder to discern. (The Tokyo Round of the GATT may best be interpreted as a "successful" *stemming* of overall breakdown in Northern trading rules rather than as an exercise in further liberalization. Rather than assessing it by calculating the (usually fairly marginal) gains from modest tariff cuts, one ought to be considering a counterfactual case of a major (catastrophic?) retreat from agreed trading principles and practices, although this is certainly less easy to write publishable papers about.) On the other hand, a collection of Southern and Eastern non-members will do their best to deal on their own terms, and collectively so whenever they can manage it, with the Northern "centre". In trading and other relationships, the North and the South will discriminate against one another; the South seems much less likely to develop as a unified bloc, however, and will probably itself remain more divided within itself than the North.

Conclusion

That "orthodox" economic theory does have considerable power to elucidate the issues surrounding North-South debate over protectionism and trade in manufactured products seems indisputable. Generally speaking, its deployment is likely to be helpful to Southern positions. Its real analytical power is not, however, in the simple popular bromides concerning "free trade" and comparative advantage so much as in the understanding it can bring to such matters as market failure, informational and other imperfections, trade internalization, concentration, and the "distortions" of every kind which require analysis of the second-best. Those parts of economics usually offered in programmes in "industrial organization" or in *general* economic theory are more likely to be useful in this respect than are those conventionally offered in today's postgraduate courses in "international trade" theory.

While the crude tenets of comparative advantage theory may be immediately helpful to the Southern cause in the context of current debate over protectionism in the North, the writing of new safeguard clauses in the GATT and the like, the use of a more sophisticated theoretical approach to markets and their mal- and non-functioning in particular circumstances is likely in the longer run to be still more helpful. "Free trade fetishism" is generally found together with general "market fundamentalism". If there are ultimately to be attempts to curtail restrictive business practices and abuses of positions of dominant market power, and otherwise to transfer to the international plane the governmental monitoring and regulatory practices which are considered normal at the national level, one must select one's arguments with care. It is probably wiser *not* to encourage the more romantic and naive conceptions of the inadequately schooled as to the efficacy of "free" international markets, lest they give strength to arguments in other spheres and on future occasions for total global-level *laissez-faire*.

References

Baldwin, R.E. 1980. "The Political Economy of Protectionism" (mimeo).

Baldwin, R.E. & Murray, T. 1977. "MFN Tariff Reductions and LDC Benefits under the GSP", *Economic Journal,* March 1977.

Baldwin, R.E. & Mutti, J.H. 1973. "Policy Problems in the Adjustment Process (U.S.)", in H. Hughes (ed.), *Prospects for Partnership, Industrialization and Trade Policies in the 1970's.*

Bhagwati, J. 1971. "The Generalised Theory of Distortions and Welfare", in J. Bhagwati et al., *Trade, Balance of Payments and Growth.* North-Holland.

Caves, R.D. 1974. *International Trade, Investment and Imperfect Markets.* Princeton, International Finance Section. Special Papers, No. 10, November.

Chenery, H.B. 1961. "Comparative Advantage and Development Policy", *American Economic Review,* March 1961.

Corden, M. 1974. *Trade Policy and Economic Welfare.* Oxford.

Corden, M. 1975. "Costs and Consequences of Protection: A Survey of Empirical Work", in P. Kenen (ed.)*International Trade and Finance, Frontiers for Research.* Cambridge.

Diaz-Alejandro, C.F. 1975. "Trade Policies and Economic Development", in P. Kenen (ed.) *International Trade and Finance, Frontiers for Research.* Cambridge.

Dunning, J.H. 1979. "Explaining Changing Patterns of International Production: In Defence of the Eclectic Theory", *Oxford Bulletin of Economics and Statistics,* November, 1979.

Ethier, W. 1979. "Internationally Decreasing Costs and World Trade", *Journal of International Economics,* February, 1979.

Finger, J.M. & Yeats, A.J. 1976. "Effective Protection by Transportation Costs and Tariffs: A Comparison of Magnitudes", *Quarterly Journal of Economics,* February, 1976.

Giersch, H. (ed.) 1979. *On the Economics of Intra-Industry Trade.* Tubingen.

Helleiner, G.K. 1981. *Intra-firm Trade and the Developing Countries.* Macmillan.

Helleiner, G.K. 1979. "World Market Imperfections and the Developing Countries", in W. Cline (ed.), *Policy Alternatives for a New International Economic Order, An Economic Analysis.* Praeger.

Helpman, E. & Razin, A. 1978. *A Theory of International Trade Under Uncertainty.* Academic Press.

Isard, P. 1977. "How Far Can We Push The 'Law of One Price'?", *American Economic Review,* December, 1977.

Jenkins, G., Glenday, G., Evans, J. & Montmarquette, C. 1978. "Trade Adjustment Assistance: The Costs of Adjustment and Policy Proposals" (mimeo).

Jones, R.W. 1977. *Two-ness in Trade Theory: Costs and Benefits,* International Finance Section, Princeton University, *Special Papers* No. 12, April 1977.

Lavergne, R.P. 1981. "The Political Economy of U.S. Tariffs", Ph.D. dissertation, University of Toronto.

McCulloch, R. 1973. "When Are a Tariff and a Quota Equivalent?". *Canadian Journal of Economics,* November, 1973.

Murray, T., Walter, I. et al. 1978. "Alternative Forms of Protection", *Kyklos.*

OECD 1980. *The Impact of the Newly Industrializing Countries on Production and Trade in Manufactures.*

Pomery, J. 1979. "Uncertainty and International Trade", in R. Dornbusch & J.A. Frenkel (eds.) *International Economic Policy, Theory and Evidence.* John Hopkins.

Sampson, G.P. 1980. "Contemporary Protectionism and Exports of Developing Countries". *World Development,* February, 1980.

Shackle, G.S. 1955. *Uncertainty in Economics and Other Reflections.* Cambridge.

Stern, R. 1975. "Testing Trade Theories", in P. Kenen (ed.) *International Trade and Finance, Frontiers for Research.* Cambridge.

Takacs, W. 1978. "The nonequivalence of tariffs, import quotas and voluntary export restraints", *Journal of International Economics,* November, 1978.

Tumlir, J. 1977. "Can the International Economic Order be Saved?", *The World Economy,* October, 1977.

Wolf, M. 1979. "Adjustment Policies and Problems in Developed Countries", World Bank Staff Working Paper No. 349, August 1979.

Wolf, M. 1980. "Tower of Babel: Conflicting Ideologies of Adjustment", *The World Economy,* February 1980.

Chapter 4

Trading Rules, Market Forces and Government Policies

Stein Rossen

Introduction

This paper is divided into two parts: the first part attempts to bring out the incompatibility between an international trading system based on the free play of market forces and the national economic systems organized under the auspices of sovereign States, an incompatibility which has become more pronounced to the extent that the play of market forces has given rise to transnational corporations (TNCs), i.e., decision-making centres operating at the international level. The focus is on the developed market economies (DMEs), in view of the fact that the trading system was designed by these countries to serve their needs and also because the truly mixed character of the DMEs tends to be overlooked in international discussions, not least by these countries themselves.

The second part of the paper discusses certain features of the search for a new international economic order (NIEO) related to the establishment of new rules and mechanisms designed to control or modify the operation of market forces. Attention is drawn to the role of two types of major actors, the governments and the TNCs, and to the need for at least some coordination at the intergovernmental level of policies of structural change related to the international division of labour and the patterns of growth.

Two additional points may be made by way of introduction. The first is that Part I of the paper does not distinguish sharply between the period of rapid growth of the DMEs and the subsequent years of crisis and stagflation in these countries. The reason for this is that, while the crisis was triggered by an unusual constellation of forces, it had roots in the past. In fact, the international trading system as well as the national economies were under increasing strain in the years preceding the 1973/75 recession. The major features of the DMEs did not change in recent years, but the problems encountered became much more difficult to handle, once continued rapid growth could no longer be taken for granted. The second point is that the focus on trading rules reflects the emphasis on structural change in production and trade. The monetary and trading systems need to be consistent and mutually supportive; monetary reform, including essential improvements in the overall adjustment process, can facilitate the solution of, but not resolve, issues pertaining to interrelated structural change and adjustment in the world economy.

The discrepancy between theory and practice — the case of the DMEs

The postwar trading system centred on GATT was designed as a liberal system calling for non-intervention by governments and for conduct of trade by private enterprise in competitive conditions. In particular, selective intervention by governments was to be limited to tariffs, which were to be reduced over time. Competitive conditions were expected to approach those stipulated by neoclassical theory, although the General Agreement, contrary to the Havana Charter, did not contain any provisions for the control or elimination of restrictive business practices.

Towards the end of the 1950s, the DMEs could conclude that their efforts to achieve trade liberalization and currency convertibility had been successful, although a number of hard core restrictions remained in agriculture and certain traditional industries. At that time, the discussion of West European cooperation had already focused on the issue of economic integration in the shape of Customs Unions and Free Trade Areas. The liberalization on a sub-regional basis within EEC and EFTA was followed by the Kennedy Round, which brought about substantial reductions of tariffs of manufactured goods on an MFN basis. However, during the entire period of expansion, selective intervention by governments in their national economies was widespread and on a massive scale, not only in agriculture but also in industry.[1] Thus, while the trading rules resulted from the victory of the free trade ideologists in the controversy about the postwar international economic system, the views of the "planners" tended to prevail in the management of most national economies.

As pointed out by Myrdal in his Cairo lectures,[2] the free play of market forces can tend to cause inequality rather than equality. Governments of industrialized countries have endeavoured to offset this tendency through regulatory policies designed to protect weak regions and people, sometimes — as in the case of agriculture — defined by reference to sectors of economic acitivity. This general trend towards government intervention was strengthened in the postwar period, which witnessed the growing importance of the public sector and the gradual acceptance by most governments of new ideas of indicative planning and new methods of policy-making with a view to pursuing, in addition to the more traditional welfare-oriented goals, short term and longer term objectives of employment and structural change.

The maintenance of high levels of employment, related not only to national policies of demand management but also to the US balance-of-payments deficits, was accompanied by a growing preoccupation with the management of supply by means of selective policy instruments. In general terms, the objectives of supply management were to ensure continued expansion through the removal of bottlenecks, the promotion of investment in promising areas ("picking the winners" or positive adjustment policies) taking into account prospective development at home and abroad, and the support of rationalization and consolidation of industrial branches experiencing difficulties in the face of foreign competition ("rescuing the losers" or defensive adjustment policies).

According to the OECD secretariat, industrial policies were essentially growth and efficiency oriented during most of the postwar period, but in recent years of stagflation, positive adjustment policies have given way to negative policies.[3] However, during the period as a whole, DMEs have pursued defensive or negative policies in respect of traditional industrial sectors, such as textiles, clothing and leather goods, including footwear. More generally, adjustment related to intra-OECD, and in particular intra-West-European, trade has tended to be more positive than adjustment related to trade with Third World countries, in view of the fact that the DMEs have become interdependent in a very concrete sense through the gradual establishment of an intricate network of intra-branch trade in processed inputs as well as finished manufactures.

The increasing concentration of private economic activity in the postwar period was brought about by economies of scale — in R and D, production, marketing, finance and information — associated with technological change and competition in terms of new products, publicity and servicing. This trend manifested itself in national economies as well as in the world economy, where it was associated with the internationalization of production in response to such factors as commercial policy barriers, servicing requirements, cost differentials among countries, and growing possibilities of disaggregating production processes. Industrial activity was also increasingly characterized by the co-existence of competition and cooperation; the latter involved cooperation among large firms, often in the area of technology, between small and medium-sized firms, frequently for defensive purposes, and between small and large firms, with the former typically serving as the sub-contractors of the latter.

The trend towards concentration was often promoted by governments, through efforts to bring about consolidation of individual industrial branches, through incentives offered to TNCs envisaging the possibility of establishing subsidiaries in their countries and, more generally, as a result of their planning endeavours in the area of investment and structural change. Although governments remained in principle committed to competition, the concentration of economic power was as a rule assessed in terms of its impact on the performance of the national economy. Restrictive business practices, including abuse of dominant market power, affecting the trade of other countries, remained largely uncontrolled, with one major exception, EEC intra-trade.

The maintenance of full employment during the period of expansion was associated with improved job security and other benefits, which are highly desirable in themselves but tend to slow down shifts in employment and, hence, to reduce the ability of the economy to adjust to change, including changes required by the maintenance of an open trading system. Moreover, pay and income settlements, involving also people in sectors and professions subject to State regulation, have become increasingly difficult in the highly organized DME societies, each group aiming at least at maintaining its earnings in relation to those of other groups while resisting any decline in pay in real terms.

Another important feature of the DMEs was the downward inflexibility of administered prices. Productivity increases in strong sectors producing internationally tradable goods, as well as in sectors not exposed to foreign competition, were as a rule reflected in higher factor payments; increases in labour and other costs were, as far as possible, passed on to prices, and changes in relative prices tended to be associated with a rise in the average price level. Together with the tendency for pay increases to be general and approximately of the same order of magnitude throughout the economy, these informal rules of the game in the area of pricing cannot but contribute to inflation.

The characteristics of the processes of wage and price formation largely explain the reluctance of governments to rely on devaluation as a means of bringing about adjustment. The introduction of floating exchange rates in 1973 failed to improve the process of adjustment, not only because of the volatility of uncontrolled capital flows but also owing to inadequate responses to changes in relative prices.

Governments were also increasingly constrained in their policies by two other factors, viz. the high trading ratios resulting from the very process of trade liberalization and the emergence of the TNCs as another major actor in investment and trade. In the absence of international coordination, high trading ratios complicate demand as well as supply management. Efforts have been made to coordinate demand management at economic summits of major powers as well as under the auspices of the OECD. But coordination of supply management, i.e., of policies of structural change and adjustment, has not yet been attempted at the intergovernmental level. Effective international coordination in both areas, and especially in the latter, would involve concerted efforts to control or influence the policies of the TNCs, which have privileged access to credit on the international market, maintain their own internal pricing systems and, in general, can respond to economic events, including changes in government policies, by altering the allocation of functions among their existing subsidiaries and by modifying their investment plans.

In the course of the period of increasing difficulties, starting at the end of the 1960s, the maintenance of the international competitiveness of the national economy, and in particular that of domestic industry, seems to have become a matter of overriding concern to governments. This development has, in turn, been accompanied by an increase in the bargaining strength of enterprises at the expense of labour, accommodation of new or soft values only to the extent that the competitiveness of industry is not adversely affected, and participation, active or defensive, in the international technological race, spearheaded by the TNCs. More recently, governments seem to have become less inclined to intervene selectively in their economies: "picking the winners" appears to be more complex than in the past, while certain policies of "rescuing the losers", such as the use of subsidies to support current earnings, are considered more carefully than a few years ago, when expectations about an early recovery still prevailed. However, the main features of the DMEs, as described above, are most likely to persist, as indicated, *inter alia,* by some of the results, or lack of results, of the multilateral trade negotiations (MTN) conducted under the auspices of the GATT.[4]

The new code on subsidies and countervailing duties recognizes the importance of subsidies as a policy instrument. Account is of course also taken of the fact that the use of subsidies by one country may cause injury to the interests of its trading partners. But the code as a whole conveys a definite impression to the effect that the DMEs will continue to rely on subsidies, and especially on domestic or production subsidies, as a means of attaining particular policy objectives. An important feature of domestic subsidies is that they affect exports as well as imports; the illustrative list of such subsidies includes grants, loans and guarantees, fiscal incentives and government financing of R and D.

It is equally relevant to note that the MTN failed to achieve agreement on safeguards against increasing imports of particular products (referred to in the MTN as the Multilateral Safeguard System), a policy area which, according to the Rey Report, was characterized already in 1972 by the absence of international discipline.[5] The key issue was that of selectivity, i.e., application of restrictions on a discriminatory basis. The DMEs did not have a uniform position on this issue, but virtually all West European countries favoured selectivity, presumably because of their reluctance to apply measures which could disturb intra-trade among themselves. At any rate, the acceptance of selectivity would tend to limit safeguard action to cases where increasing imports of a particular product can be attributed to newcomers rather than to well-established suppliers. Further negotiations on safeguards are envisaged; in the meantime, GATT members would "continue to abide" by the existing provisions,[6] i.e., those which had failed to impose any discipline in the past.

These current features of the DMEs do not correspond to the assumptions underlying neoclassical theory. This fact was clearly recognized in a report published by the OECD secretariat in 1970,[7] according to which "it is by no means easy to devise a consistent policy" under modern conditions, since the core of the theory "is based on such 'ideal' assumptions as perfect competition, transparency of markets, perfect foresight, constant returns to scale, complete divisibility, consumers' sovereignty etc.". The report goes on to state "such assumptions are hardly appropriate to a world where as much as half of the final output is not really governed by market mechanisms (public sector, nationalized or State-regulated industries, agriculture, a part of services and housing); where, of the remainder, about half again is under the direct or indirect control of a few big firms; where advertising and demonstration effects are predominant in shaping consumer preferences; where information is both imperfect and costly; and where government influence in its various forms is extremely wide''.

The search for a new international economic order

The principles, objectives and directives for further work embodied in the resolutions adopted by the General Assembly in 1974 and 1975 constitute a new departure in the North-South Dialogue by shifting the emphasis from improvements in the existing international economic order to the establishment of a new order. In particular, these resolutions brought out sharply a number of key issues within a general framework relating existing economic and social inequalities to the distribution of power and bargaining strength within the world economy. Indeed, changes in the power structure were seen as a prerequisite for the achievement of equity and social justice. Thus, the resolutions assert the principle of the sovereignty of States over the natural resources within their borders; request the introduction of more democratic processes of international decision-making; emphasize the need for control and regulation of the activities of TNCs in investment, technology, production and trade, and call for greater efforts by the developing countries (DCs) to generate countervailing power through various forms of cooperation between governments, organizations and enterprises of the Third World.

In the area of commercial policies defined by reference to the General Agreement (GATT), the break with the past was much less sharp. Thus, the resolutions emphasized the need for substantial improvement in the access of DCs to the markets of the developed countries and for special and more favourable treatment for DCs, including a larger degree of freedom for these countries, individually as well as in their intra-trade, in the use of commercial policy instruments for development purposes. However, more emphasis than in the past was placed on the need to supplement commercial policies by measures reflecting a "managed" approach to trade expansion among DCs. Moreover, attention was drawn to the use by DMEs of selective industrial policy instruments other than those falling under the traditional heading of commercial policy. As regards the latter, industrialized countries were requested to develop new policies and to strengthen existing policies with a view to facilitating the industrialization of the DCs by means of appropriate structural adjustments.

A number of negotiations in most areas relevant to the NIEO were launched in the context of the North-South Dialogue in the wake of the sixth and seventh special sessions of the General Assembly, with a view to establishing an international institutional framework conducive to development and structural change. One common feature of these new negotiations, e.g., those regarding the integrated programme for commodities, the revision of the industrial property system, the code of conduct on the transfer of technology, and the principles and rules for the control of restrictive business practices, was their concern with the operation of market forces, which they sought to control or modify through the adoption of new rules and mechanisms. The resolutions of the General Assembly also aimed at highlighting development objectives, or introducing such objectives, in the ongoing negotiations on changes in the existing trading and monetary rules, which are mainly designed to regulate the conduct of governments. Finally, the second half of the 1970s has witnessed intensified activities in the area of economic cooperation among developing countries (ECDC), which has been increasingly seen both as a means for the implementation of the NIEO and as a desirable feature of that order. As a means, ECDC is to serve two major, interrelated objectives, viz. (i) to achieve a substantial increase in mutually beneficial economic interchanges among DCs, and (ii) to build up organized economic strength in the Third World and common negotiating positions *vis-à-vis* the developed countries.[8]

The new global negotiations mentioned above have proved to be time-consuming and difficult. For the purpose of this paper, some comments will be made on the negotiations within UNCTAD on the code of conduct for the transfer of technology and the principles and rules for the control of restrictive business practices. Agreement on the latter set of principles and rules was reached in April 1980; substantial progress has been achieved in respect of the technology code, but several issues were still outstanding at the close of the third session of the negotiating conference in May 1980. Both instruments are concerned with the control and regulation of market forces, taking into account the existing unequal distribution of market power and bargaining strength. However, while the principles and rules deal only with the prevention of restrictive practices, the technology code is also concerned with "positive" aspects, i.e., ways and means of facilitating transfer of technology and building up the technological capabilities of DCs.

The set of principles and rules for the control of restrictive business practices is not legally binding, and takes the form only of recommendations. However, the strength of the instrument is enhanced by its endorsement by the General Assembly and, in particular, by the inclusion of provisions for consultations, cooperation and exchange of information among States, as well as for continued consideration at the intergovernmental level under the auspices of UNC-TAD of restrictive business practices within the framework given by the principles and rules.

While the substantive parts of the set of principles and rules are complex, reflecting compromises that lend themselves to different interpretations, the objectives are fairly straightforward, being basically free trade and competition oriented in accordance with neoclassical theory. Thus, the principles and rules are, *inter alia,* framed "to ensure that restrictive practices do not impede or negate the realization of benefits that should arise from the liberalization of tariff and non-tariff barriers affecting world trade" and "to attain greater efficiency in international trade and development" such as through "the creation, encouragement and protection of competition" and "control of the concentration of capital and/or economic power".

The objectives just quoted should be seen in conjunction with the fact that, given the power structure, the DCs should benefit from the mutually reinforcing action called for at national, regional and interregional levels, "to eliminate, or effectively deal with, restrictive business practices, including those of transnational corporations, adversely affecting international trade, particularly that of developing countries and the economic development of these countries". Moreover, the instrument provides for preferential or differential treatment for DCs "in order to ensure the equitable application of the principles and rules". The provision says that, in controlling restrictive business practices, States should take fully into account "the development, financial and trade needs of developing countries, in particular the least developed countries". In this connexion, the provision refers to the establishment and promotion of domestic industry and the encouragement of economic development through regional or global arrangements among developing countries. For the purpose of building up countervailing power, the DCs may also take advantage of (i) the exclusion of intergovernmental agreements from the scope of the instrument, and (ii) another provision stating that in the application of the principles and rules account should be taken of the extent to which the conduct of enterprises "is required by States". These two provisions are, of course, also of interest to both categories of developed countries.

A major issue in the negotiations on the principles and rules concerned the relations among enterprises under common control, e.g., belonging to a TNC. The DCs insisted on wide coverage and relatively strict control also in the case of restrictions "within the family", while the DMEs were unwilling to cover such restrictions except in very limited circumstances. On the one hand, the TNCs, especially those engaged in vertically integrated operations, are considered by DMEs as being rational and efficient, *inter alia* because they bring a number of enterprises under common management. On the other hand, the very exercise of common management involves many, if not all, of the practices which as a rule are considered as anti-competitive when carried out under formal or informal agreements concluded among independent enterprises. Faced with this dilemma, efficiency considerations have prevailed. Thus, according to an OECD expert group, "competition laws and policies in the OECD member nations generally provide that intra-enterprise practices, such as allocations of functions among branches or subsidiaries of a single enterprise, are not in themselves considered as unreasonable restraint of trade. Holding such practices unlawful would be likely to discourage internal growth and decrease efficiency".[9]

The issue of intra-TNC transactions was solved by means of two separate articles. The first states that enterprises, except "when dealing with each other in the context of an economic entity wherein they are under common control, including through ownership, or otherwise not able to act independently of each other", should refrain from practices which "limit(s) access to markets or otherwise unduly restrain competition, having or being likely to have adverse effects on international trade, particularly that of developing countries, and on the economic development of these countries". A number of such practices are listed. The second article, which deals with abuse or acquisition (e.g., through mergers, take-overs and joint ventures) and abuse of dominant market power, lists a number of acts or types of behaviour, and it applies, whenever relevant, also to intra-corporate transactions. Whether such acts or behaviour are abusive or not should be examined by reference not only to the criterion or criteria applied in the first article, but also to a number of other criteria set out in a complex, interpretative note. Although TNCs would be subject to more scrutiny than in the past, it seems most likely that the bulk of their activities, in particular those that are technology-intensive and vertically integrated, will remain centrally managed and that, consequently, these enterprises will continue to function as international decision-making centres.

As already noted, substantial progress has been achieved in respect of the technology code, but several important issues are still outstanding, including that of its legal character. The agreed draft preamble, objectives and principles contain broad indications of the philosophy of the envisaged instrument. Thus, these parts of the code, *inter alia,* (i) draw attention "to the need to improve the flow of technological information ... in particular ... on the availability of alternative technologies, and on the selection of appropriate technology suited to the specific needs of developing countries"; (ii) call for the encouragement of "transfer of technology transactions, particularly those involving developing countries, under conditions where bargaining positions of the parties are balanced in such a way as to avoid abuses of a stronger position and thereby to achieve mutually satisfactory agreements"; and (iii) state that technology-supplying parties "should respect the sovereignty and the laws" of the technology-acquiring country and "endeavour to contribute substantially to the development" of that country.

A large measure of agreement has been reached in respect of the identification of 14 objectionable restrictive practices, but the approach of the DMEs has differed from that of the DCs. While the former seek to avoid practices that restrain trade, the latter are primarily concerned with practices hampering the economic and social development of technology-acquiring countries. The difference in approach is also reflected in the frequent recourse of group B to "the rule of reason", while the 77 prefer precise rules designed to eliminate the restrictive practices, subject to the insertion of an escape clause according to which the competent national authorities of an acquiring country may decide to disregard a practice proscribed by the code provided that, on balance, there will be no adverse effect on the economy of that country. Finally, the negotiations have revealed widely divergent views on the extent to which the provisions regulating restrictive practices should apply to intra-corporate transactions.[10]

Various attempts have been made to solve the issues related to "the rule of reason", the escape clause, and intra-corporate transactions by means of a "chapeau" to the chapter of the draft code on restrictive practices. As regards the TNC issue, the texts put forward are in certain respects similar to the text agreed at the conference on restrictive business practices. The failure so far to reach an agreement in the area of transfer of technology reflects the relatively sharp conflict of interest between technology-supplying and technology-acquiring countries.

Substantial progress has been achieved in respect of the text setting out the responsibilities and obligations of parties to transfer of technology transactions. The draft lists the positive elements to be considered in the negotiating phase and in the contractual phase. The parties should, in general, be responsive to the economic and social development objectives, particularly of technology-acquiring countries, and observe fair and honest business practices. A specific provision states that the potential supplying party should, upon request by the other party, make adequate arrangements as regards "unpackaging in terms of information concerning the various elements of the technology to be transferred, such as that required for technical, institutional and financial evaluation" of his offer.

The technology code is not likely to become a legally binding instrument, as desired by the 77. In exchange, however, agreement has been reached on provisions designed to promote action to implement the code at the national level and to ensure monitoring of the code at the international level through the establishment of appropriate international machinery within UNCTAD.

Given energetic follow-up at the intergovernmental level, the principles and rules for the control of restrictive business practices, as well as the regulatory part of the technology code (when agreed), should contribute to greater equity in international economic relations. The positive elements of the technology code would also facilitate the elaboration and implementation of active self-reliant development policies by the governments of DCs. However, neither of these instruments is designed to deal directly with the key issue of structural change related to the international division of labour and patterns of growth in the world economy.

Industrial studies indicate that in the course of the next two decades, there may be an extensive redistribution of world industry, both geographically and among sectors, in response to technological developments, changes in the competitive positions of countries, and other factors.[11] The extent to which, and the manner in which, this restructuring will take place depends in no small measure on the policies and reactions of the two main actors: the governmentes and the TNCs.

Arguments are frequently put forward to the effect that governments of DMEs should shift to more neutral policies designed to in-

74

crease the flexibility of their economies, with a view to facilitating structural change consistent with an international division of labour based on comparative advantage. The result would be a move out of many production lines of traditional industry, associated with simultaneous rapid growth of advanced industrial sectors such as electronics and capital goods. In practice, governments of most industrialized countries are not likely to let the output of their traditional industries fall below a certain share of domestic consumption. As regards the advanced industries, on the other hand, governments — in particular those of larger countries — will most probably continue to pursue active policies of support, for security as well as economic reasons, through the financing of R and D programmes, active participation in trade promotion, and other measures. These policies, which tend to accentuate the technological race, are not likely to maximize human welfare. Moreover, most DCs have good reasons to oppose an international division of labour which would leave them with traditional industries and labour-intensive processes of modern industries managed by the TNCs of the developed countries.

The relations between governments and TNCs involve cooperation as well as actual and potential conflicts. Home countries, almost exclusively DMEs, are likely to weigh the benefits of an increase in the competitiveness of their TNCs resulting from investment and production abroad against the actual or potential decline in their share in the value added. On the other side, the host countries, DCs as well as DMEs, will attempt to exploit the decision-making power of the TNCs to their advantage, e.g., through performance criteria in terms of domestic value added and exports. In recent years, developing countries have become better equipped to negotiate with TNCs; they have also been assisted in their endeavours by the increasing competition among TNCs of different home countries. But the odds remain against them, in view of their dependence on the technology and the marketing channels of the TNCs.

As noted in Part I, the processes of structural change and adjustment are not at present subject to any coordination or concerted action on the part of governments. This applies to their own policies, to those of the TNCs and to the interplay between the two. Such coordination or concerted action should ideally take place within a framework of rules and criteria designed to promote development while avoiding or minimizing conflicts among nations. This is admittedly a tall order not only because of the substantive problems involved but also in view of the reluctance shown so far by governments to discuss other than commercial policies in international fora. But there seems to be a growing recognition of the need for a new departure, as shown by the conclusions reached by the expert team in charge of the OECD Interfutures Project,[12] as well as by suggestions put forward by the UNCTAD secretariat.[13]

The OECD team favours market mechanisms and free trade, but it recognizes fully the roles of governments and TNCs in the past and expects these two actors to continue to play their roles in the future. Thus, according to the team, the development of international trade may be governed by two trends, viz., a growth of trade within TNCs and increasing government intervention. In the opinion of the team, new forms of concerted action or cooperation among governments are required to promote structural change while avoiding excessive disturbances, e.g., the emergence of substantial surplus capacity, which might provoke government reactions jeopardizing the open trading system. Decision-making by governments as well as by enterprises should be facilitated by means of the establishment of an industrial information system and the examination of industrial adjustment problems at the world level on the basis of sectoral studies carried out with the cooperation of major enterprises in relevant fields, a recommendation that is reminiscent of indicative planning practices at the national level. Finally, the team concludes that the improvement of the functioning of international markets would also require "new rules of the game and codes of conduct both for enterprises and governments".[14] The contents of the new rules and codes of conduct are not spelled out, but the conclusion implies that the team does not consider existing OECD instruments as adequate for the purpose of managing structural change.

The UNCTAD report draws attention to the persistence of structural and institutional rigidities in the DMEs and to the inconsistency between the market-oriented rules of the game and the reduced role of market prices in determining the allocation of resources within the national economies. The report further notes that the reconciliation of conflicting national objectives is difficult, if not impossible, in the context of slow growth and structural disequilibria and suggests that planned structural changes would be needed in order to break away from the vicious circle of instability, recession, inflation, and payments imbalances. Such changes would involve large investments on a worldwide scale, requiring collective action focused on the development of the Third World by the international community as a whole. The operational conclusions of the report, which was submitted to

UNCTAD V, called for the establishment of a high level advisory group assisted by small working or study groups, as appropriate, for the purpose of (i) examining the problems related to the management of the world economy, especially policies in the fields of trade, payments and finance and their relationship to development; (ii) assessing the consistency of those policies with longer-term development objectives; and (iii) recommending, for consideration at the intergovernmental level, concerted measures that would promote structural changes in the world economy and thus provide a favourable environment for sustained development at the global level.[15] The Conference took no action on this suggestion.[16]

The reports published, resepctively, by OECD and UNCTAD, differ, as would have been expected, in several respects, e.g., in value premises, focus and approach. However, they have also important aspects in common. Thus, both reports recognize the mixed nature of the DMEs, the need for structural change and adjustment, and the inadequacies of the existing international rules and mechanisms. Another common aspect is that they do not provide more than broad indications of the directions of further work.

The UNCTAD report might be said to reflect the view that a start could be made by providing a forum for pragmatic, high level discussions and consultations on development objectives and related structural change, taking into account all relevant policies as well as the depressed state of the world economy. The discussions and consultations would draw upon all suggestions put forward with a view to improving the functioning of the world economy, covering concerted action in key areas as well as new rules of the game. As regards the latter, it follows from the line of analysis and reasoning of this paper that new rules of the game are not likely to be observed if their purpose is to ensure "neutral" government policies and competition among enterprises in accordance with neoclassical theory. Any new set of rules should therefore provide for mechanisms for action at the intergovernmental level to achieve at least some degree of consistency, not only in the area of global management but also in respect of structural change related to government policies, TNC policies, and to the two sets of policies taken together. Efforts to coordinate policies have of course to serve certain objectives, which should not be limited to the avoidance of excessive disturbances in the world economy but be directly related to the promotion of economic and social development and to human welfare generally. Action along these lines should not divert the attention of DCs from the crucial area of cooperation among themselves. Indeed, concrete progress in ECDC will contribute to, and most probably be a condition for, development-oriented achievements at the global level.

Notes

1 OECD, *Inflation — The Present Problem,* December 1970, page 49.
2 Gunnar Myrdal, "Development and Underdevelopment, A Note on the Mechanism of National and International Inequality", Cairo 1976.
3 OECD, *The Case for Positive Adjustment Policies,* 1979, pp. 71—81.
4 MTN Studies, No. 4, Report prepared by John E. Jackson for the U.S. Senate Sub-Committee on International Trade (Washington, 1979), draws attention to two approaches, one designed to minimize government interference, i.e., the original GATT approach, and another related to the ideas of "organised free trade" and "dirigisme". According to Professor Jackson (page 5), the overall results of the MTN "have many features which suggest more of the second approach than of the first".
5 OECD, *Policy Perspectives for International Trade and Economic Relations,* 1972, page 82.
6 GATT, *The Tokyo Round of Multilateral Trade Negotiations,* January 1980, page 42.
7 OECD, *The Growth of Output 1960—1980,* page 140.
8 Rules and mechanisms of ECDC would constitute additions to, and — whenever required — changes in, the present "rules of the game". A first medium-term plan for global priorities was adopted at the Ministerial Meeting of the Group of 77 at Arusha in 1979. Since that time, meetings of DCs at regional as well as inter-regional levels have been convened to consider three priority projects, viz. a global system of trade preferences among DCs; the establishment of multinational marketing enterprises of DCs; and the elaboration and implementation of various forms of cooperation among state-trading organizations in the Third World.
9 Restrictive Business Practices and Multinational Corporations (para. 200), OECD, 1977.
10 See the above comments on this issue in the case of the principles and rules.
11 OECD, *Facing the Future,* 1979.
12 *Ibid.*
13 TD/225, Policy issues in the fields of trade, finance and money and their relationship to structural change at the global level.
14 OECD, op. cit., page 414. Taking into account other parts of the report, it would appear that the team is primarily concerned with the question of new rules for TNCs.
15 TD/225, page 21.
16 The Conference did, however, adopt a resolution on protectionism and structural adjustment pursuant to which the Trade and Development Board has decided to carry out annually a review of the patterns of production and trade in the world economy with a view to identifying elements or problems most relevant, in the light of the dynamics of comparative advantage, to the attainment of optimum overall

economic growth, including the development and diversification of the economies of developing countries, and an effective international division of labour. In carrying out the review, account was to be taken of "all relevant available information, including general policies". However, the first review (September 1980) failed to open the door for a realistic examination of problems of structural change.

Part II

International Trade Theory and Southern Industrialization Practice

Chapter 5

Industrialization, Technical Change and the International Division of Labour

Frances Stewart*

One important element of the NIEO is the endorsement of the Lima declaration, which laid down a target for the international division of labour — that one quarter of world industrial production should be located in the Third World by the year 2000. There was, it seems, little sophisticated justification for the figure selected; rather it represented an ambitious yet possibly feasible target[1] based on less developed countries' (LDCs') belief that industrialization was essential for a sustained growth in incomes, to improve the terms of trade, and to achieve economic independence. The Lima target has — if realized — a number of important implications for development, but these depend on the *form* industrialization takes — its distribution between different LDCs and the nature of the industries that develop — as much as on its total quantity. The effects on growth, on poverty, and on the terms of trade vary according to the form of industrialization. This paper considers some of the determinants of industrial location and the international division of labour. It explores how far "conventional" theory gets in explaining and analysing Third World industrialization and considers how recent work on technological change, as well as insights into political factors, affect the analysis.

Existing theory may be divided into four categories:

(i) conventional theory "proper" — or neoclassical theory;
(ii) the "technological" explanations of trade and the division of labour, developed in response to the weakness of neoclassical theory in dynamic terms. These include technological gap (Posner), product cycle (Vernon), and Linder's theories;
(iii) theories incorporating product differentiation and economies of scale;
(iv) cumulative causation theories.

* *I am grateful for comments on an earlier draft to participants at the Refnes Seminar, especially G.K. Helleiner, and to S. Teitel.*

We shall briefly discuss each category, considering its realism and relevance to the question of industrial location and development strategy. The final section draws some tentative conclusions about the direction of innovations in economic theory needed to deal more fully with the question of industrial location and the international division of labour.

(i) *Neoclassical theory* states that industries will be located in accordance with countries' comparative advantage deriving from factor endowment. Consequently LDCs will tend to specialize in activities in which they can employ natural resources and in labour-intensive industries. There are three important respects in which the theory has to be qualified.

First, there exist non-economic restrictions on location (e.g., tariff and non-tariff barriers); for brevity we usually describe these as political determinants, although this does not do justice to the issues, since the restrictions flow from political economy, rather than politics; they arise because of the desire and power of various groups to secure economic benefits for themselves (Diaz-Alejandro 1978). While the existence and implications of such restrictions have long been recognized, it is only recently that it has been demonstrated that they should not be taken as given from outside the system but are themselves the product of forces within the economy, and subject to analysis by social scientists. Thus, Helleiner (1977) distinguishes between "new" and "old" protectionism, and shows that protectionism is more likely where there is an identity of workers' and capitalists' interests, and less likely where capitalists in developed countries (DCs) benefit from free trade (as with the "runaway" industries and big retail buyers). (See also Turner *et al.,* 1980.)

Secondly, efficiency of production is not simply a matter of some particular combination of capital and labour. At its simplest the theory assumes that all countries operate on the same production function for each commodity, and thus comparative advantage/location is just a question of comparative costs. But it is well known that total factor productivity varies greatly even with precisely the same technology and even in the same economy (Salter 1960). Differences between economies are greater, as noted and described in a general way by Leibenstein in his concept of X-efficiency. Hirschman noted the difference between DCs and LDCs and argued that they were in part due to managerial differences, being least in "machine-paced" activities. Tests of his hypothesis have established the general fact that there are big differences between productivity in industries using similar technologies in DCs and LDCs. For example, in a study of seven Latin American countries and 37 different categories of manufacturing industry, Teitel shows that in every case average labour productivity in the Latin American industries was a fraction of that in the USA, ranging from 13 percent to 81 percent, but typically being less than a half. Most of the tests of the hypothesis have supported the Hirschman view that the differences in productivity are least in (variously defined) machine-paced activities. However, not all studies find this to be a convincing explanation, while in each case a good deal of the variation in productivity remains unexplained.[2]

The Leibenstein concept of X-efficiency is rather too general to be very useful, while Hirschman offers only a partial explanation. Further analysis of the phenomenon suggests that total factor productivity of a given technology is likely to vary according to infrastructure (see Doyle's comparison of cement plants, 1965), managerial factors, general industrial experience of the labour force, experience in that particular industry, and experience with that particular technology (see the work of Katz and associates, 1978), and the level of education and skill of the labour force.[3] It follows that there are likely to be differences between different LDCs — as well as between LDCs as a group and DCs — and that the differences will be greater, as Hirschman (1958) noted, for some industries than for others. Much more work is needed to establish the extent of differences and their causes. But we already know enough to believe that, far from there being a single production function shared by all, *each country will have a unique production function* — showing output obtainable with differing technologies — and that the production function of each country will change over time with changes in the various factors that determine it, quite apart from the general phenomenon of technological change. This is a very important conclusion, from the point of view of international trade, and one that has not been properly incorporated into trade theory. It means, first, that a country's comparative advantage is not simply a function of factor endowments of capital and labour but of all these other factors too; secondly, that what it chooses to do today will influence its performance tomorrow. Neoclassical theory has partially incorporated the first point by adding "human capital" to the production function and specifications of factor endowment. But to the extent that differences are due to infrastructure, economies of scale, and experience (for which formal education is no substitute), "human capital" does not properly describe them. Moreover, since much of the relevant "human capital" is a product of industrial experience rather than formal training, it is an outcome as well as a cause of decisions on industrialization.

Different technologies impose different resource requirements — not simply in terms of capital and labour, but in terms of requirements for skill of various kinds, technological and social infrastructure and so on. (Stewart 1977, chapter 1). For example, technologies are often described as "science-based" or not, or "machine-paced" or not. Each of these distinctions is rather crude and arbitrary; and other distinctions need to be added (e.g., use of energy). A full description/classification of industries would probably do away with these distinctions and contain a ranking of the various relevant requirements the technologies have. The important point is that each technology is associated with a *set* of requirements, and the productivity of that technology in any particular environment will depend on how far these requirements are met.

In a parallel fashion, each country (or potential industrial location) possesses, at one point in time, access to a set of resources, each at a certain price. The total factor productivity of any technology depends on the extent to which the resources to which a particular location has access matches (in quality and quantity) those that are required. The relative costs of production depend on the costs of these resources as well as factor productivity. Thus, assuming unrestricted location decisions, industrial location and the international division of labour will depend on how far and at what price different countries possess the various resources the different industrial technologies require. In the context of modern industry, capital/labour requirements may be of subsidiary importance as compared with management, industrial experience of the labour force, and the other factors mentioned above.

Thirdly, while so far (along with neoclassical theory) we have assumed a static technology with a given set of characteristics, and a technology that is equally accessible throughout the world, technology is actually changing continuously. Moreover, accessibility to new technologies is imperfect and depends on (a) the origins of the change; (b) market imperfections — legal and other — in the technology market; and (c) the skills, experience and knowledge of potential acquirers of technology. With *changing* technology, the ability to acquire and adapt to the change becomes an important ingredient of industrial success. Since industries vary in the speed and significance of technological change, the extent of change becomes a relevant industrial characteristic and the ability to keep up with change a relevant resource in determining industrial location. Technological change means a change in the resource requirements of each technology and thus can influence industrial location — e.g., by reducing/increasing the relative use of unskilled labour. Neoclassical trade theoreticians, when they incorporate technological change in their models, typically assume that it occurs "neutrally" — i.e., it has no systematic resource-using bias. But the nature of technological change is influenced by the *origin* of that technological change, since it is designed for use in the particular economic/technological/social circumstances where it is designed (Salter 1960, Atkinson and Stiglitz 1969, Stewart 1977). Technological change originated in DCs thus tends to be increasingly capital-intensive, skill and science-using, etc. Technological change originating in LDCs tends to be more appropriate for LDCs in term of the characteristics of production techniques and of products.

The theory of "dynamic comparative advantage" rescues conventional theory in a purely tautological sense, stating that comparative advantage changes over time as technology changes, but since it does not incorporate any theory of the nature of technological change or of its transmission, it ceases to be a comprehensive theory determining the international division of labour.

(ii) *The technological theories,* of which that featuring the "product cycle" (Vernon 1966, 1979) is best known, were developed in recognition of the significance of technological change in explaining industrial location. According to the product cycle theory, technological change occurs in DCs, where initial production takes place, but once the technology is "mature" the lower labour costs in less developed countries cause production to be located there, while the advanced countries introduce new industries based on new technological advances. This theory contains an important truth, but is is weak in three assumptions:

(i)   the theory assumes that each industry goes through a simple and similar progression to maturity and that the point of maturity is obvious;
(ii) that at maturity the industry will be pushed out to LDCs, irrespective of the state of maturity of the LDC economy;
(iii) that all technological change takes place in DCs and LDCs are simply passive recipients.

87

Recent work on technological change challenges all three assumptions. In many industries, technological change is continuous; in others it occurs in jumps. Few industries follow the simple product cycle pattern. In most there is an almost continuous succession of "vintages" of technology, while the older vintages may or may not become obsolete according to changes in the nature of products, technologies, and other economic circumstances. Thus, there is no simple distinction between the mature and the immature. Moreover, LDCs' ability to use the technologies varies (on the lines described above) in accordance with their experience, and industrial and scientific skills — so there is a hierarchy of technologies of varying degrees of "maturity" and also a hierarchy of countries with varying capacities to use the technologies. Moreover, the imperfect technology market intervenes in the process, making transfer much more difficult (perhaps impossible) in some cases and easy in others. Further, trade restrictions inhibit or prevent some product cycle exports.

Recent work on industrial performance in LDCs has indicated that in some cases LDCs are not simply the passive recipients of technology but adapt it, and indeed initiate changes which they then sell to others (Katz *et al.* 1978, Lall 1981). Yet in other cases, no local technological change is initiated (Bell 1980). Whether or not local adaptation takes place is important in determining efficiency, in both static and dynamic terms. It is therefore important to understand why it takes place in some situations and not in others. Bell has suggested some negative influences — including the degree of protection, lack of technical expertise and relevant experience; the work of Katz *et al.* has suggested positive factors, including "push" factors, which make it difficult to operate at all without adaptation, and facilitating factors, like experienced technical personnel. More systematic research is needed to differentiate factors conducive to local adaptation and to explore how far such activity is an important aspect of eventual industrial efficiency.

Technological adaptation and change originating in LDCs qualifies and may undermine the product cycle approach, which essentially describes a continuous wave of DC-LDC technology transfer. LDC technology change has even occasionally involved reverse transfer, while it at the same time offers other LDCs new sources of technology. However, DC research and development — sometimes in response to restrictions and protection — may also change the nature of the technology in such a way as to retain, enhance, or even *re*-establish DC locational advantages, thus, again, undermining the process of the product cycle (as, for example, in the electronics and parts of the textiles industries, Turner *et al.* 1980).

The product cycle theory describes how new products are developed, and then relocated. But it says very little about what happens to *old* products. While some new products add to the total, most displace existing products. Consequently, those producing the old products find their markets are diminishing. Thus to maintain/increase industrial production, markets have to be maintained, either by producing the new products, or by finding new markets for the old products. The need to update products underlines the need to adapt to change; markets for old products may sometimes be maintained by moving into low-income Third World markets.

(iii) Theories incorporating *product differentiation and economies of scale* were developed to explain the large and growing amount of trade between similar economies, often within the same industry (Grubel and Lloyd 1975). Neither the neoclassical nor the technological gap theories offer a sufficient explanation. The neoclassical trade paradigm suggests that trade should be least between similar countries (because of similarities in factor endowment and consequently in comparative advantage) and greatest between dissimilar countries. Yet in practice the reverse is the case, with most trade in manufactured products occurring between rather similar advanced countries. The technological "gap" explanation of trade (Posner 1961) offers one explanation of this, suggesting that temporary technological leads are responsible for trade among similar advanced economies. But such leads are, according to Posner, *temporary,* and trade will be eliminated once advanced countries catch up in the relevant technologies, which they tend to do in quite a short time. Thus a continuous and growing quantity of leads and lags in technological advance would be necessary to explain the rapid growth in trade between advanced countries. Moreover, trade also occurs within industries where no obvious technological leads and lags are involved; for example, similar but differentiated final products are exchanged, e.g., Volvos and Fords, while different parts of the same final product are often made in different countries. In both these sorts of trade — differentiated final products and intermediate products — it is hardly possible to rely on either the neoclassical or the technological explanations. The factor endowment in the various countries involved is normally similar; for example, in the production of Ford motor cars in Europe all production takes place in similar advanced countries. Other cases have been noted where production all takes place in various somewhat similar LDCs, e.g., in car production in Latin America. Moreover, there is no obvious technological gap in knowledge of production techniques of the various final products; nor can there be with respect to production of intermediate products, where a multinational corporation is responsible for all parts of the production process and can transfer its technological knowledge to any location it wishes.

Product differentiation *cum* economies of scale have been suggested as explanations of intra-industry trade between similar economies. (See Ethier 1979, Krugman 1979, Lancaster 1980.) The relevant economies of scale are those associated with increased division of labour, on the lines of Adam Smith's pin example. The productivity of each operation in the production process tends to increase as specialization and the length of production runs increase. But as specialization increases, different parts of the process of production need not be carried on under the same roof (i.e., in the same plant), nor necessarily in the same firm or even in the same country.

The existence of economies of scale above a certain threshold is sufficient to explain international trade between similar economies. For differentiated final products, where there is a market for a number of similar but differentiated products, the existence of economics of scale implies that any one country may find it is only economic to produce a limited number of the total products marketed and to import the remainder. Similarly, international trade in intermediate products may take place to exploit economies of specialization and division of labour. The theory does not explain why any particular pattern of country and industry specialization occurs; it simply states that some trade will be advantageous, given the existence of economies of scale. Theoretically, if we assume identical production functions for (and within) each industry, each exhibiting economies of scale, the final country specialization would be completely indeterminate, if each country started in the same position.

Once countries begin to specialize, one would expect that they would tend to do so in whole industries (including all intermediate products), because in most circumstances this would minimize transport costs, and because of the organizational problems involved in having intermediate products located all over the world. Yet, as noted, trade in intermediate products is very important. It is worth while exploring possible reasons for this. First, different parts of the productive process of any final product may differ in their factor use, and factor prices differ between countries, especially as between

DCs and LDCs. The resulting cost differences can be important enough to overcome the transport cost factor, and they provide the explanation for the "runaway" industry type of intra-industry specialization and trade, in which labour-intensive parts of the productive process are located in LDCs (Helleiner 1973). But this does not help in explaining the statistically much larger phenomenon of inter-DC intra-industry trade. Second, as far as the organizational problems of internationalization of sourcing are concerned, they are substantially reduced where the same firm (the multinational corporation) is responsible for the whole productive process. The very large importance of intra-firm trade is well established (Helleiner 1981). It seems likely that a significant proportion of intra-industry international trade occurs where the multinational corporation is responsible for each element of production, and where production is not divided between a number of independent firms.

Countries do not start in the same position, but start with a particular set of industries, accumulation of knowledge, extent of specialization, etc. When economies of scale are important, where countries start determines where they go; and this is even more significant if we also allow for learning economies (not formally part of this group of theories). Thus this set of theories, as they stand, cannot explain industrial location, only that some trade will take place. These theories are not therefore themselves sufficient to answer the sort of questions posed by the Lima target — as to the likely quantity and nature of LDC industrialization and trade. To determine this, the starting point is vital. Defining any one point of time, say 1980, as "the starting point" for each country, different countries begin in different places for a variety of reasons. These include geographic/climatic differences; cultural differences; "accidents" of history, e.g., particular interventions by governments, influences of migrants, etc; and differences in the general level of development, as measured, for example, by the size of the manufacturing sector.

The last point is of obvious particular relevance to the position of LDCs, and is at the centre of the last category of trade theory.

(iv) *Cumulative causation* theories (Myrdal 1956, Griffin 1979) emphasize the significance of both economies of scale and learning by doing, stating that productivity depends on the accumulation of skills, and on internal and external economies of scale. This extremely important point, which lies behind many of the criticisms of the neoclassical theories made earlier, underlines the significance of the starting point to the determination of a country's comparative ad-

91

vantage. In itself, however, the cumulative causation theory hardly constitutes a theory of industrial location, since it says nothing about any factors other than cumulative experience.

Some conclusions for Third World industrialization

Each of the theories discussed offers some insights into issues of industrial location and trade. For example, despite its deficiencies, it is clear that the neoclassical approach emphasizes one important source of comparative advantage and of trade for LDCs — *viz.,* their advantages in labour-intensive industries. Similarly, it has been shown that the product cycle is a powerful explanation of aspects of international investment and trade (Hirsch 1967, Vernon 1979). But — with the exception of the cumulative causation theories — none of the theories fully incorporates learning effects and therefore the importance of a country's industrial history into an explanation of its capacity to produce and compete. The product differentiation/economies of scale school of thought incorporates *static* economies of scale. But these are different from learning economies, or increases in productivity arising from the accumulation of experience, which are sometimes described as dynamic economies. In practice, of course, they may be confused because they often occur simultaneously, since to achieve a large scale of production (and therefore static economies of scale) normally involves a large accumulation of experience (and therefore dynamic economies). The difference between the two is that in the case of static economies each country potentially operates on the *same production function,* with its productivity depending on where it operates on that production function, i.e., on the scale of production. Thus any country — developed or underdeveloped — could, if it set up a sufficiently large plant, benefit from the same static economies of scale and compete with equal productivity with other producers of similar size in other countries. If the size of market is limited to domestic sales, then countries are initially unequal because of unequal size of markets, but with international trade the world market becomes a potential market for each producer, so that this source of inequality is removed.[4] In contrast, a theory incorporating dynamic learning effects finds that every country operates on a different production function, its productivity depending on the accumulation of experience and skills historically, as well as on the scale of production at one point in time. The omission of the significance of historical experience in determining productivity and therefore competitiveness is of greatest significance where there are marked differences in experience between countries. It is therefore of much greater relevance to discussions of North-South trade than to discussions of trade between historically similar economies.

It is apparent then — from this very brief review — that while all four groups of theories contain important insights, none is sufficient to explain and predict the international division of labour in a dynamic world where development is uneven. To be able to determine this, just for one industry, we need to know:

(i)   the requirements of the technology for conventional resources (labour, capital, energy, etc.), infrastructural requirements, managerial, scientific and technical demands, the importance of industrial experience (in general and in particular) in determining efficiency, as well as the ability of different economies to supply the various requirements;
(ii) how the technology is changing — the speed of change, and the direction of change; whether technological change in LDCs will be likely to increase their capacity to compete, or whether DC technological change may lead to technologies which the DCs can operate best and which undermine LDC activities;
(iii) how markets are changing and how this affects the relative competitiveness of old and new technologies;
(iv) actual and changing restrictions on location, e.g., tariff and non-tariff barriers in DCs, restrictions by raw material or energy producers in LDCs.

The analysis above has emphasized the importance of learning — industrial and technological skills — in determining comparative industrial efficiency. We need more empirical information on the nature of this learning process, its magnitude, and the extent to which it is industry-specific, or is mainly a matter of general industrial experience. The significance of learning — both general and technical — suggests that just as industries can be represented in a sort of hierarchy representing varying scientific/technical requirements for efficient operation,[5] so countries can also be ranked hierarchically in their ability to operate technologies of varying degrees of scientific/technical sophistication. As countries move up this hierarchy, through education and experience, so their productivity in modern industries rises from near zero (complete incapacity to operate) to something approaching DC levels. They become competitive in a particular industry at the point at which their rising productivity means that DCs' productivity advantage is no longer so great that it outweighs their greater factor costs. The further accumulation of experience which occurs at this point gives rise to a further rise in productivity and may lift the country to the break-even competitive point in a more sophisticated industry. Thus a process of cumulative and increasing competitiveness occurs — which may explain the spectacular success of some countries at a certain point in their development (e.g., Taiwan, South Korea in the 1960s and 1970s). This cumulative process is likely to continue (as shown in the diagram) until the rapid expansion of employment increases labour costs. As labour costs rise, the speed with which the LDC in question displaces DC activities is likely to be reduced, while other LDCs — at an earlier stage of development — may begin to displace the original LDC in the least sophisticated lines.

The diagram illustrates the argument for one industry. In the diagram LDC labour costs are much below DC costs, but initially this is more than offset by the low labour productivity in the LDC so that unit labour costs in the LDC far exceed those in the DC. However, as experience is accumulated, labour productivity rises and unit labour costs fall, until a 'break even' point is reached where DC and LDC costs are equal. From then on with the further accumulation of experience LDCs become progressively more competitive, compared with the DC. The accumulation of experience and rising labour productivity tend to affect other industries too. Productivity in a particular industry is a function of general industrial experience (as well as other factors), not just experience in one industry. Consequently, the position of the labour productivity curve for each industry, and the break-even point, are likely to be affected by what is happening in other industries. Eventually — as shown in the diagram — the industrial expansion exhausts the labour surplus, and LDC wages rise.

In this particular case, international competitiveness can only be achieved after an initial period of experience during which LDC costs substantially exceed international costs. The case for industrial protection rests on this. Industrial protection is essential in the initial stages; this protection need not take the form of tariffs, but could consist of subsidies and other encouragements. Whether protection should be specific to particular industries, at a high rate, or generalized over all industry at a low rate depends on whether and to what extent the learning effects are industry-specific, which is an empirical question likely to vary between different types of industries, and per-

Diagram

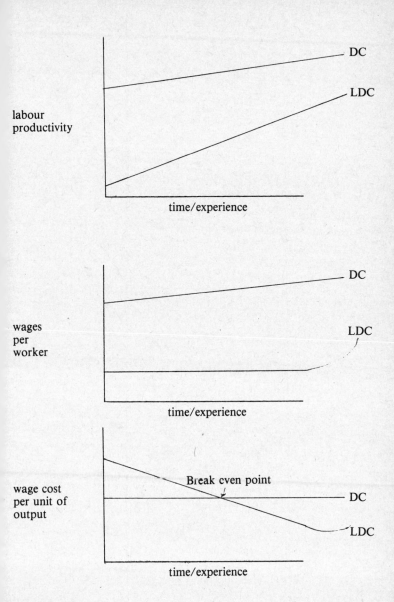

haps also countries. Industries may be ranked according to labour or capital intensity. This ranking gives one ordering for introduction of industries in LDCs, and (roughly) that which would follow from a free trade/international price approach to industrial development. There are two other orderings of relevance: one is ranking according to scientific/technological requirements; another is ranking according to potential learning effects. Conflicts between criteria for industrial selection occur where these rankings differ. The neoclassical approach to industrial development tends to give zero weighting to learning effects, while the heavy protection strategies (e.g., in India) tend to give prime emphasis to learning and little to static comparative advantage. Choices between criteria may be due to differences in objectives, but they are also, it seems, due to differences in opinion about the relevant empirical relationships — in particular, the importance of learning, and how far it is industry-specific.

The effect of industrialization on income distribution and poverty within any LDC is likely to vary according to the form of industrialization, and its speed. More labour-intensive/simple-product types of industrialization are likely to involve a more equal pattern of income distribution. But the labour-intensity/product type depends not just on choice of technique/product in a static sense, but also on how the technology is changing over time. Reliance on DCs for the major part of new technologies — on product cycle lines — means adopting increasingly capital-intensive technology over time. Local technological innovation is necessary to avoid this. But local technological innovation requires local technological and capital goods capacity, which in turn requires considerable industrial experience. Thus there may be a conflict between the short run and long run: short run employment-maximizing policies could involve a choice of industries (light consumer goods) that have few learning effects and do not build up the capacity for long-run technological innovation. Local LDC technological innovations are not necessarily (although they are likely to be) more "appropriate" than technology imported from DCs. Much depends on the local environment, including factor availability and price, and, particularly, markets and product requirements. Local innovation may be of three types: it may make adjustments to imported technologies, to increase its local efficiency — leaving the major characteristics of the technology to be determined by technology imports; it may permit the continuation of old vintages of technology by maintaining its competitiveness; or it may involve major innovations into new lines. There are examples of all three types in LDCs, but the first two seem to be most common (which is as one would expect, since one or the other is probably a necessary precursor of the third type). The first type does not do much to increase the appropriateness of technology or products. (Many of the examples studied by Katz and associates (1978) are of this type). The second does increase appropriateness (this seems to be the type common, for instance, in India and historical Japan); while the third (of which there are few examples) could potentially do so. Thus the LDC environment determines whether local LDC technological capacity does, in practice, increase appropriateness.

The effect of industrialization on poverty in the Third World depends critically on the country distribution of that industrialization. The neoclassical model would suggest that all poor countries could participate in labour-intensive industrialization; similarly the product cycle model does not differentiate between technology recipients. But the learning model suggests that capacity to produce industrially is likely to vary with experience and with scientific and technical resources. It follows that there is likely to be an uneven distribution of industrialization, with countries that are more advanced in scientific/technological capacity industrializing more rapidly; those that do industrialize more rapidly are likely to increase their competitiveness, through the learning process, and move up in the hierarchy of industries in which they compete. It follows then that a process of cumulative inequality in the distribution of industry among LDCs is likely. Countries that start in an unfavourable position initially can only offset this by very heavy industrial protection or promotion. Eventually, the more successful LDCs will move into a labour-scarce situation, giving a competitive edge to lower wage competitors. But many LDCs (e.g., India) could expand industrially for a very long time before this happened. Thus the NIEO policy of industrialization is likely to increase inequality within the Third World, as between countries, and also in many cases within countries.

A major justification for the industrialization policy was to escape the poor terms of trade believed to be an inevitable consequence of specialization in primary products: the Prebisch thesis. But there has been little attempt to consider what happens to the *industrial* terms of trade as LDCs move into industrialization, from either a theoretical or empirical point of view. From a theoretical point of view, it is necessary to consider whether the reasons for expecting poor (and/or worsening) terms of trade for primary product specialization, were

97

aspects of primary production as such, or general features of the LDC economy, compared with those of DCs. Recent analyses of the (labour) terms of trade (e.g., Emmanuel 1972, Lewis 1978) suggest that poor terms of trade are the consequence of low wages, and are thus likely to be features of industrial production as much as primary production. Hence LDC industrialization is not likely to avoid poor terms of trade in the short or medium term.[6] Only measures which reduce the labour surplus and/or increase real wages are likely to be effective in improving the labour terms of trade. Returns to capital and technology form another element in the overall terms of trade. Work on the terms of technology transfer has shown that the terms tend to be worse for the recipient the greater the monopolistic elements present and the more science-based the industry. Where LDCs import their technology, they do not avoid poor terms of trade by local production. Only if advanced country monopoly/oligopoly power in relevant products and technology is removed, or at least eroded, by Third World technological development, is this aspect of the terms of trade likely to improve.

It thus appears that the industrialization aims of the NIEO are not likely to be effective, in the short run, in reducing poverty, or in improving the terms of trade. Nor is the third aim — increasing independence — an obvious immediate consequence, since industrializing countries remain dependent for management, technology, parts and markets. But the learning aspects of industrialization suggest that the consequences may all prove different in the long run, for certain forms of industrialization. Industrialization *cum* technological development (which cannot occur without industrialization) gives countries the capacity to choose an alternative development path, which could enable countries to meet all of these objectives.

Notes

1 The Third World's share of industrial output was roughly 6% in 1960 and had risen to 9% by 1977. UNIDO calculates that if 1960—75 trends continued, the Third World's share of industrial output in 2000 would be substantially below (about one half) the Lima target, but if GDP growth in the Third World was 2% above historical trends and growth in the rest of the world 1% below historical trends then the Lima target would be achieved. See Singh (1980) and UNIDO (1979).
2 The conclusions of the tests of the Hirschman hypothesis are summarized by Teitel (1981) and Bhalla (1976).

3 White suggests that — at least as far as labour-intensity is concerned — it is associated in Pakistan with the degree of competition (1976).
4 Ethier assumes the international market is available to each producer.
5 This hierarchy is likely to accord (broadly) with the date of origin of the technology, the more recent being more sophisticated (science-based).
6 Hans Singer (1950) was also the originator of a Prebisch type thesis of deteriorating terms of trade for primary products (which is sometimes known as the Prebisch-Singer thesis), but in his "revisit" (1975), Singer agrees with the argument put forward above — *viz.*, that "To put the point differently, Singer I assumed the central/peripheral relationship to reside in the characteristics of *commodities,* i.e., modern manufactures versus primary commodities. Singer II now feels that the essence of the relationship lies in different types of *countries"* (p. 376).

References

Atkinson, A.G. & Stiglitz, J.E. 1969. "A New View of Technological Change", *Economic Journal,* 78.
Bell, R.M. 1980. "Learning and Technical Change in the Development of Manufacturing Industry: A Case Study of a Permanently Infant Enterprise" S.P.R.U. Sussex.
Bhalla, A.J. 1976. "Low-Cost Technology, Cost of Labour Management and Industrialization", in N. Jequier (ed.) *Appropriate Technology — Problems and Promises,* O.E.C.D.
Diaz-Alejandro, C.F. 1978. "International Markets for LDCs — the Old and the New" *American Economic Review,* 68.
Doyle, L.A. 1965. *Inter-Economy Comparisons: A Case Study,* University of California Press.
Emmanuel, A. 1972. *Unequal Exchange: A Study of the Imperialism of Trade,* Monthly Review Press.
Ethier, W. 1979. "Internationally Decreasing Costs and World Trade", *Journal of International Economics,* 9.
Felix, D. 1977. "The Technological Factor in Socio-economic Dualism: Toward an Economy of Scale Paradigm for Development Theory" *Economic Development and Cultural Change,* 25, Supplement.
Griffin, K. 1979. *International Inequality and National Poverty,* Macmillan.
Grubel, H. & Lloyd, P. 1975. *Intra-Industry Trade,* Macmillan.
Helleiner, G.K. 1973. "Manufactured Exports from Less Developed Countries and Multinational Firms", *Economic Journal,* 83.
Helleiner, G.K. 1977. "Transnational Enterprises and the New Political Economy of U.S. Trade Policy", *Oxford Economic Papers,* 29.
Helleiner, G.K. 1981. *Intra-Firm Trade and the Developing Countries,* Macmillan.
Hirsch, S. 1967. *Location of Industry and International Competitiveness,* Clarendon Press.
Hirschman, A. 1958. *The Strategy of Economic Development,* Yale.
Katz, J. 1978. "Technological Change, Economic Development and Intra and Extra-regional Relations in Latin America", IDB/ECLA Research Programme in Science and Technology, Working Paper No. 30.

Katz, J. et al. 1978. "Productivity, Technology and Domestic Efforts in Research and Development", IDB/ECLA Working Paper, No. 13.

Krugman, P.R. 1979. "Increasing Returns, Monopolistic Competition and International Trade", *Journal of International Economics,* 9.

Lall, S. 1981. *Developing Countries in the International Economy,* Macmillan.

Lancaster, K. 1980. "Intra-Industry Trade under Perfect Monopolistic Competition", *Journal of International Economics,* 10.

Leibenstein, H. 1966. "Allocative Efficiency vs. X-Efficiency", *American Economic Review,* 56.

Lewis, A. 1978. *The Evolution of the International Order,* Princeton.

Linder, S.B. 1961. *An Essay on Trade and Transformation,* Almqvist and Wicksell.

Myrdal, G. 1956. *Development and Underdevelopment,* National Bank of Egypt Fiftieth Anniversary Commemoration Lectures, Cairo.

Posner, M.P. 1961. "International Trade and Technical Change", *Oxford Economic Papers,* 13.

Salter, W.E.G. 1960. *Productivity and Technical Change,* Cambridge.

Singer, H.W. 1950. "The Distribution of Gains between Investing and Borrowing Countries", *American Economic Review.*

Singer, H.W. 1975. "The Distribution of Gains from Trade and Investment Revisited", *Journal of Development Studies,* 11.

Singh, A. 1980. "Industrialization in the Third World, de-industrialization in advanced countries and the structure of the world economy", Dept. of Applied Economics, Cambridge.

Stewart, F. 1977. *Technology and Underdevelopment,* Macmillan.

Teitel, S. 1981. "Productivity, Mechanisation and Skills: A Test of the Hirschman Hypothesis for Latin America", *World Development,* 9.

Turner, L. et al. 1980. "Living with the Newly Industrializing Countries", Chatham House.

UNIDO 1979. *World Industry Since 1960: Progress and Prospects,* New York.

Vernon, R. 1966. "International Investment and International Trade in the Product Cycle", *Quarterly Journal of Economics,* 80.

Vernon, R. 1979. "The Product Cycle Hypothesis in a New International Environment" *Oxford Bulletin of Economics and Statistics,* 41.

White, L.J. 1976. "Appropriate Technology, X-Inefficiency and a Competitive Environment: Some Evidence from Pakistan", *Quarterly Journal of Economics,* 90.

Chapter 6

Comparative Advantage, Efficiency and Equity in Collective Self-Reliant Industrialization

Ricardo Ffrench-Davis

Two simultaneous, though widely divergent, analytical developments have been taking place in the sphere of international economic relations. On the one hand, free trade approaches have been gaining ground in the conventional literature and in the actual economic policies of some LDCs, particularly in the southern cone of Latin America. On the other hand, there have been renewed efforts geared toward the design of collective self-reliant strategies for the Third World.

The first set of approaches has been reinforced by the growing fashionability of the monetary approach to balance of payments analysis, which emphasizes the long-run aspects of adjustment of the external sector, in developed homogeneous economies (Johnson 1976).[1] This extremely abstract theory has been mechanically transferred to some LDCs, and policies based upon it are actually being implemented. One crucial component of the overall approach is the recipe of free trade and free capital movements, in order to foster commodity and financial arbitrage. In the conventional set of proposals, market comparative advantage, without any of the well-known and widely accepted qualifications developed in the fifties and sixties, appears as the indisputable resource allocator.

One component of collective self-reliant strategies (CSR) is the promotion of reciprocal trade among LDCs. Formal processes of economic integration are the mechanisms that have received most attention in the literature. But these processes include only some few LDCs. Alternatively, a generalized system of trade preferences among Third World countries has been suggested, subject to two requirements: survival of special preferences among members of regional groupings and protection for the economically weaker members (UNCTAD 1975, p. 58).

In this paper I want to bring together three strands of analysis: (i) cooperation among LDCs, (ii) distributive issues, and (iii) efficiency considerations. I claim no originality, except, perhaps, for the effort to examine them in conjunction one with another.

The framework of the analysis

It is common to treat each economic problem separately. If this treatment were a good reflection of reality, it might be easy to solve each of them by "first best solutions". However, the fact is that the reality of LDCs (and even DCs) is extremely complex, with multiple sources of disequilibria and various forms of interdependence among them; moreover, disequilibria are made up not only of marginal imbalances or distortions, but usually also of structural deviations from "equilibrium".

When one is dealing with economic cooperation among LDCs (and also of course, in trade relationships with developed economies), the specific design and implementation of the process may have crucial implications for equity and efficiency. Rather than the conventional theory recipe of allowing the market to operate freely, and then redistributing income by lump-sum transfers, the existence of multiple disequilibria lends support to direct forms of intervention in the market, which may improve efficiency and eventually guarantee an equitable distribution of benefits.

What is discussed below is relevant for a variety of forms of economic cooperation: comprehensive processes of economic integration; production arrangements among large LDC producers of a given basic commodity, geared to foster the selective production of some of its inputs and capital goods; preferential trade agreements among all LDCs, or groups of them, covering all trade or some sectors or a limited number of commodities. For the sake of simplicity, we will use the expressions of "economic integration" or "economic cooperation" to describe that whole family of collaborative actions.

It may be redundant but it is nonetheless important to stress that CSR strategies do not imply autarchy (Fortin 1978, Corea 1977), but a drive away from dependence and unequal exchange. CSR implies selectivity, with some role for the external as well as the domestic markets. Thus, we are back to the old dilemma of how much market intervention and how much governmental direct and indirect intervention is needed; my impression is that this question has received limited attention lately, although satisfactory answers have not yet been offered.

The distributive effects of integration appear at three different levels. Firstly, economic integration alters the foreign trade, production structures, and factor availability of the different member countries, thus conditioning the form and the degree of development which may be achieved by each of them. Secondly, the nature of the cooperation scheme itself has a decisive influence on the distribution of benefits between the group of partners and the rest of the world, with the treatment given to direct foreign investment being a key issue. Finally, the integration process affects the relative position of the different social groups and zones within each member country. Furthermore, when member countries are not well integrated internally, their participation in this process may accentuate the heterogeneity or segmentation of the national economy. This latter outcome depends on the specific characteristics of the participating economies and on the actual integration model that is used: one approach may accelerate the imitation of consumption patterns of DCs, which increases the segmentation of the national society; other approaches, as will be seen, may use cooperation to improve the feasibility of developing more egalitarian patterns of supply and demand.

The discussion will now focus on the forms that state intervention may take in strategic areas. The framework of the analysis allows for the coexistence of traditional forms of trade between LDCs and developed countries, and among LDCs themselves; it also allows for purely commercial preferential tariff arrangements for trade in certain categories of commodities. Our analysis focuses, however, on the remainder of production and trade, which includes products with "acquirable comparative advantages" and those that may have decisive distributive effects. Policies may be geared (i) to providing other LDC markets for excess installed capacities, (ii) to making use of economies of specialization in firms with diversified output, or (iii) to wholly new activities. Each of these requires some sort of common planning or coordination, which we will call "CSR investment planning".

Collective Self-Reliant (CSR) investment planning

CSR investment planning means direct intervention in the market, which may take alternative forms, each having different distributive and efficiency implications. This section examines some of the features that CSR investment planning ought to have, the role that it can play as a distributive instrument, and its repercussions upon the efficiency of resource allocation. More particularly, there is a discussion of the criteria to be used in selecting those activities which are the best candidates for programming, of the types of decisions which are suitable for centralization, and of the complementary role which central planning and the price system should play.

a) Developing countries and dynamic market efficiency

In order to avoid over-simplification, it is necessary to examine the forms that investment planning should take, if it is to represent an efficient intervention in the market. This depends upon the nature of the economy in which it will be applied.

The label of "inefficiency" that is attached by orthodox theory to all direct intervention in the market rests on the assumption, among others, that potential producers have a clear knowledge of the "comparative advantage" which a country enjoys. In practice, however, there are two common problems which are met in trying to identify those economic activities with comparative advantage. Firstly, there exist, in developing economies, numerous market disequilibria and distortions which mean that current market prices do not reflect the social scarcity or availability of productive resources. A typical example — and one of the easiest to identify — is the under- and unemployment of labour. Such imbalances establish differences between market and social (static) comparative advantage.

Secondly, even if market prices correctly reflect the current social scarcity of resources, there are, in fact, thousands of goods and of relative prices, and their great number makes it difficult for the investor to have certain knowledge of which products will enjoy comparative advantage when his investment matures.[2] It is not surprising, therefore, that investors generally place great weight on the near past (Arrow 1974, p. 6) and on the tendencies currently prevailing in the market, at the expense of dynamic considerations.

A public investor may, of course, experience the same difficulties. Thus, the important point lies not in the relative efficiency of public and private investors, which depends on other factors, but in the fact that in the framework described above, the market is not operating optimally. There is, as a result, room for intervention in the market, even allowing for a margin of error, so as to increase its overall efficiency. In this case, intervention in the market has the double purpose of helping to make comparative advantages more easily recognizable and of actually generating them, in those sectors in which they depend principally upon characteristics which may be acquired during the production process itself or upon the selection of areas of specialization (Stewart 1981, Westphal 1980).

In order to illustrate the implications of these characteristics of developing economies as regards the relationships between redistribution, market intervention, and efficiency, let us consider two examples of "diffuse comparative advantages". One relates to existing activities and the other to new investment alternatives.

(i) The experience of many developing countries has shown that, in their import substitution processes, there has been a failure to take advantage of potential economies of scale. So as to make the best out of their situation, enterprises have diversified their production in an effort to increase the rate of utilization of their installed capacity. As this phenomenon has been repeated in various countries, the result has been unnecessary and costly duplication of investment and of the variety of products in the output mix throughout the industrializing areas. When attempts are made to integrate these markets, there exists the possibility of creating competition as a result of which enterprises located in some countries may go bankrupt, whereas those located in others may completely take over the markets in the area. This instance of what is known as "trade creation" tends to have a severe effect upon distribution, destroying sources of employment which it would be difficult to replace in the short term, and producing resistance to the integration process, which would be damaging to its political viability.

An alternative to a straight-forward liberalization of the exchange of these commodities consists in the adoption of "specialization programmes" which would regulate the specialization process within each enterprise. Given the prevailing diversification of products, it is possible for each enterprise to improve its productivity by specializing in a smaller number of varieties (intra-industry specialization among countries), each of which would begin to be produced in larger quantities once the firm acquired access to partners' markets. It is clear that it is not easy to implement such a system but, on the other hand, neither has it been easy to liberalize the reciprocal trade of "conflictive" goods; in addition, specialization programmes, as long as they avoid unnecessary unemployment and uncertainty during the adjustment process, can be more efficient.

Apart from the obvious cases where there is plant obsolescence or where the relative availability of the standard factors of production, natural resources or transport costs play a decisive role, it is difficult to determine which products and/or which varieties have "comparative advantage", since this can evidently be acquired. There is no unique optimal solution. A key element as regards cost reduction in integration schemes is the selection itself of a pattern of specialization which differs for each plant. To the extent that "economies of specialization" are significant, it will be possible for the gains which they bring to compensate for the mistakes contingent upon distributing specializations among enterprises, and for the expenses involved in the administration of economic cooperation.

The selection of product varieties may have implications for demand patterns. As long as the structure of supply influences that of demand, and that seems to be the case within certain limits, the process of specialization may seek more standardized consumption. In the political sphere this needs, obviously, a redistributive will on the part of authorities in the participating countries. In the economic sphere, it would be facilitated by direct actions on demand patterns (e.g., non-market distribution of commodities and import controls) or indirect intervention via price incentives and regulation of advertising.

Clearly, centralization is necessary in carrying out the process of allocating specialization patterns. The role of producers in this process may range from that of merely providing information to one of actual decision-making. Moreover, the process may allow the continuing independence of the enterprises, or it may result in their integration into some type of multinational firm formed by member countries. In practice, the instrument of centralization that is used to decide on specialization patterns has so far most commonly been that of existing transnational corporations, with obvious distributive implications for the host countries. In the case of integration processes, the already existing presence of branch offices of the same corporation in several of the countries about to become integrated will probably lead to a greater specialization on the part of each of the subsidiaries. Consequently, if member countries are to retain a significant proportion of the benefits resulting from specialization, economic policy must be geared towards regulating the operation of transnational companies.[3] Alternatively, centralization has sometimes been achieved through the formation by powerful private economic groups of large holdings or mergers, or by the organization of public enterprises.

In those cases where the enterprises operating in each country are independent of one another, it is necessary to create a centralized locus for decision-making, either endowed with executive powers or serving as the venue for negotiations among the national authorities, with or without the direct participation of the enterprises. In order to achieve the implementation of specialization agreements, it can be stipulated that the lifting of import restrictions for a given variety will benefit only the country to which that variety has been assigned. To prevent the producer from exerting a monopolistic power, a common external tariff setting a limit on the price of the said product in the integrated market, can be established.

(ii) The existence of complementarities in investment (dynamic external economies) is a source of considerable difficulties to an isolated investor trying to assess the profitability of a specific investment (Chenery 1959). The profitability of a plant is, in fact, subject to the eventual installation of others which will complement it. Such complementarity also arises from encouragement of the production of common services, the supply of inputs, marketing channels, and specific institutions and knowledge. The planning of investment — in the sense of selecting a family of related products whose production it is intended to promote in a coordinated way — helps to provide each investor with a better defined economic framework. In fact, the joint planning of a family of products — even when investment activities are subsequently carried out by different public or private enterprises — allows a more accurate assessment than is possible in an unregulated market of the presence and magnitude of dynamic external economies and makes it possible to have a more definite idea of the prospective market.

In a sub-optimal world, with characteristics like those described above, the role assigned to the regional planning of investment is very different from that which it would play in an ideal one, where any interference would, obviously, only produce deviations with respect to the optimum and, therefore, be inefficient. In the sub-optimal real world, direct intervention, if it is relatively well carried out, may produce a movement towards the optimal static allocation of given resources and to a cumulative increase of their availability and productivity.

b) The scope of investment planning

Since examination of some of the characteristics of developing countries' markets indicates that some sorts of economic activities should be programmed, it is necessary to analyse what the range and form of investment planning should be.

The foregoing discussion itself provides the framework for the answer. The type of problem which planning must tackle has been shown to be that which concerns making "diffuse comparative advantages" more easily recognizable in a market — formed by decentralized public or private enterprises — where information is limited because of the very nature of developing economies. Implementing planning also involves practical difficulties which make it advisable to set limits to the number of products or sectors to be submitted to the process and to the type of economic decisions to be centralized. In very general terms, those decisions with greater "macroeconomic" implications should be centralized whilst those of a "microeconomic" scope should be kept decentralized.[4] Of course, the frontier between these two types of decision is also diffuse.

(i) Programmable decisions

Economic activities involve a vast spectrum of decisions which range from the assignment of the specific day-to-day tasks to be carried out in a plant to the determination of investment volume, technology to be used, and geographic location. Some types of decisions are very numerous and are of merely microeconomic implications. Therefore, it is impractical to plan them at a level higher than that of the enterprise. At the same time, and apart from these pragmatic considerations, the fact that they do not have important repercussions on the rest of the economy means that there are no technical advantages to be gained by centralizing them.

The opposite is the case with decisions concerning the geographical location of investment. The so-called "polarization" phenomenon in respect of productive activities which are geared to the servicing of the entire common market, and their associated capital and trained labour, may result in serious political impediments to the furthering of the integration process.[5] Beyond these political consequences, polarization can, in the economic sphere, lead to concentration, to a greater extent than is technically advisable, in the development "poles" of particular countries or regions. In fact, although polarization is determined partly by objective factors, it is also the result of "subjective factors", mistakes in prediction, and shortcomings in project evaluation, which may be especially likely when there are complementarities among enterprises. The spontaneous allocation of resources by the market, therefore, may suffer from inefficiencies.

Since the geographical location of regional investments clearly affects the distribution of benefits among countries and the efficiency of resource allocation, there are significant repercussions from decision-making in this regard which go well beyond the scope of an enterprise and have a bearing upon the feasibility of the integration process and upon its overall welfare effects.

From a distributive point of view, geographical location represents the most decisive variable.[6] In addition, it may also, for reasons of efficiency, be convenient to centralize marketing operations or technological research in specialized multinational firms (instead of TNCs), which would serve productive activities located in different countries. Both functions — marketing and research — are characterized by scale economies and externalities and are, therefore, potential areas for cooperation among member countries, contributing to self-reliant industrialization.

(ii) Programmable products

The number of products whose centralized programming can be efficiently undertaken is obviously limited by practical considerations. One basis for selection is to concentrate on those items whose efficient production, because of economies of scale, requires volumes exceeding domestic demand and which, at the same time, particularly require access to partner countries' markets. If products are competitive on international markets, this criterion would lose its significance; the greater the difficulties of reaching and entering external markets, the more important access to the markets of associated countries will become.

Within the framework provided by these selection criteria, it is advisable also to include related activities involving reciprocal complementarities which have significant effects upon their production costs. The potential presence of such dynamic external economies constitutes an additional criterion for selection, and indicates the disadvantage involved in carrying out planning and location only on the basis of isolated products. In other words, it suggests that products with the most significant complementarities should be grouped together. Thus, it is useful to assign "families of products" or "industrial complexes" so that the coordinated development of the various activities which they comprise will make it possible to create and to internalize dynamic external economies.

In the face of dynamic externalities, and of economies of specialization and of scale, the choice of areas in which to concentrate investment, institutional development, and industrial infrastructure acquires great importance. The larger these economies, the more diffuse the comparative advantages become and the larger the need of guiding the market toward areas on which to concentrate. Selection of areas for the concentration of activities, then, becomes crucial.

In the cases where static allocative efficiency arguments seem to carry low weight and complementarities do not offer a clear basis for choice, even a random process of such selection might be efficient for the purpose of rapidly acquiring new comparative advantages. In practice, however, protection has frequently been granted across the board. Evidence from the development strategies of some of the NICs seems to support the argument that selectivity in the promotion of industrial development is crucial to the success achieved and, in particular, to the capacity to export (Westphal 1980).

(iii) Allocation procedures

Simultaneously with the choice of commodities to be programmed there must be decisions as to which "families" of products will be assigned to which countries. In allocating each family, proper weight should be given to factors such as the avoidance of unproductive duplication, the potential for the utilization of scale, and the availability of factors and training in each participating country; these factors do not carry the same weight for all activities. Activities can, in principle, be classified according to the "comparative advantages" which they exhibit in different locations.[7] There is evidence that, in the case of many activities, the comparative advantages are indeterminate (not sensitive to location) or may be acquired during the process. As Lipsey (1976, p. 40) has pointed out, "Interference may be justified ... when we realize that many comparative advantages are acquired rather than dictated by nature". Consequently, within this context, it is possible for distributive equity considerations not to impair, and even to improve, allocative efficiency in respect of those groups of activities whose costs of production are less sensitive to their location.

The aggregate volume of allocations assigned to each country may therefore be conditioned by equity criteria, with redistributive action undertaken only in respect of those products in which the dangers of negative effects upon efficiency are low. If, however, there is an attempt to impose an equitable distribution in all productive sectors, there is danger of under-utilizing external and scale economies and of over-segmenting the market into too many producer-countries.

Thus, there is a range within which the optimum coverage of planning is bound: at the lower end, the more restricted the coverage of activities, the greater the risk of over-segmenting the market; at the other extreme, capacity to programme and to negotiate becomes a constraint on efficiency.

In practice, over-segmentation is likely to appear. It is certainly difficult to select and allocate simultaneously all the potentially programmable products. For instance, the experience of the Andean countries has shown that, owing to management difficulties and limited information, it is more viable to advance through successive approximations, programming sector by sector, one after another.[8] A sequential allocation system probably leads to excessive importance being attached within each sector to redistributive factors, since it is natural that a country should be reluctant to approve, on the basis of promises of compensation by means of allocations in future programmes for other sectors, the allocation programme of a sector which may be favourable to other countries.

On the grounds of administrative and political viability, it may, nevertheless, be necessary to operate in a sequential way. However, since the implementation of investment requires time to materialize, as the number of sectors covered by already approved programmes increases, the countries could proceed toward a balanced exchange of allocations. During this process, it would be possible to achieve greater specialization by sectors and to correct the evaluation mistakes which may have been made in the centralized process of making allocations.

c) Allocations and the complementary role of the market

The programming mechanism described above involves complementary roles for the market and for central planning. The decision as to *where* to produce is taken out of the market and the same may be done in the case of other decisions regarding such areas as the generation of technical knowledge in certain programmed sectors, the chronological sequence of some investments, and the process of marketing those products whose external market may be most difficult to penetrate. The remaining decisions — usually of a more microeconomic nature — must still be taken within the framework of each enterprise, that is, on the basis of decentralized operations and markets.

In the process of economic integration, price relationships prevailing in the market can be influenced through the harmonization of economic policies, particularly those dealing with foreign trade:

tariffs, non-tariff restrictions, government procurement practices, etc. For instance, harmonized tariff policy plays two roles in this context. It helps to ensure the effectiveness of allocation decisions and, secondly, it contributes to the appropriate utilization of allocation by the country benefiting from it, since tariffs influence the form in which the assigned article is produced and the support which that productive activity offers (or the cost it imposes) to the rest of the regional economy.

The effectiveness of allocation, in the sense that the favoured country should be the only one enabled to produce the assigned article, may be backed by the elimination, in all the associated countries, of tariffs on imports of that product originating in the designated country, while tariffs are maintained for goods originating in other member countries. For such tariff policy to be fully effective, it will usually also be necessary to harmonize procurement practices in the state sector and to establish joint policies and regulations regarding non-tariff barriers and the trading practices of TNCs (Ffrench-Davis 1979, ch. IX).

Once the designated country actually carries out the production of the assigned article, some form of regulation is advisable so that production takes place "efficiently". This involves harmonized policy as regards both sale conditions in the region and use of inputs produced within the region, that is, regional prices and regional value-added tax. An allocation represents a concession whereby the country making use of it is granted monopolistic power. This country, in fact, enjoys free access to the common market without having to share it with other regional producers. Should imports from third countries be banned, it could exploit its monopolistic position by over-charging on its sales. This tendency, which would probably be a source of conflict among partners, makes it necessary to agree, simultaneously with the allocation, on the maximum "surcharge" which the assigned country may demand, and this may be more easily regulated through an external tariff (CET). When approving an allocation and its corresponding external tariff, therefore, the other members decide on the maximum margin of preference which they are willing to grant to the nation thus favoured.[9] The rules of the game thus allow the other countries to import from third markets if the latter charge prices in excess of the CIF plus CET price. If, however, the surcharge proves insufficient because production costs (at market prices) exceed international prices by a percentage higher than the margin of preference, the assigned country could meet the difference with subsidies, so as to allow it to trade its production in the region at prices which are competitive with those of foreign imports.[10] In this way, the incentive to the production of this article is provided partly by the government of the assigned country and partly by the other partners, who agree to pay a price that may exceed the international price at most by the margin of preference.

Harmonized tariff policy can also influence the contribution which the production of assigned goods makes to the demand for inputs of a regional origin. The favoured country could otherwise unilaterally decide to encourage production by means of duty rebates for inputs from outside the region. In formal processes of economic integration, inputs may also be protected by the CET agreed for the respective items. In more limited production agreements among LDCs, it would be desirable to include some inputs in the set of assignable commodities, and to negotiate a regional margin of preference for each of these inputs. Naturally, an agreement that moves simultaneously in the horizontal and vertical directions of the process of production leads to a more "self-reliant" development, but its implementation faces correspondingly more obstacles.

Concluding remarks

The neoclassical theory of international economics offers a poor interpretation of the nature of relations between rich and poor countries. Nonetheless, the standard policy recipe of free trade is offered to all countries alike, without due consideration of their level of development and their national objectives.

The largest part of the trade flows of LDCs take place with the developed world, especially with the "market-economy" countries. Marketing, finance, advertising, technology and production are heavily influenced by transnational corporations. Collective self-reliant strategies, which run counter to the orthodox recipes, seek to introduce into the international economy more balanced relations, by fostering joint actions of LDCs in various political, cultural and economic areas. Processes of economic integration and production-trade agreements represent one such area.

Since cooperation takes place between independent political units, it must bring an equitable distribution of overall benefits and costs among cooperating countries. Reference has been made to the polarization problem that may result as a consequence of liberalization of reciprocal trade.

113

Finally, in economies undergoing a process of change toward development, future comparative advantages cannot be well defined and known, except in the cases of goods whose advantages are based upon (i) rich natural resources, climate, or geographical location, (ii) some acquired characteristic (captive technology, exceptionally skilled labour), or (iii) a significant weight of labour supply. These cases are far from covering all possible productive activities; there are many investment projects where costs and benefits depend to a significant extent upon dynamic external economies, economies of specialization, and upon the size of the markets at their disposal. In these conditions it is probable that comparative advantages will be diffuse, and the market mechanism alone unable to give a single optimal answer. The above discussion has been intended to show that, in this framework, the selective promotion of given activities contributes to the acquisition of new "comparative advantages" and to the fostering of capital formation. The argument suggests that the selection of activities, even at random, if done among activities with "diffuse comparative advantages", might be as important, and perhaps even more so, as the choice of the mechanisms to protect them, when dynamic externalities and economies of specialization and scale are large enough.

Three lines of research emerge, I believe, from the discussion. First, the criteria for the selection of areas of specialization and acquisition of comparative advantages must be explored further. A new look at the diverse experiences of NICs with respect to the criteria adopted for selecting activities to be fostered, the nature of the process of successful maturation of infant activities, the sequence of activities being promoted and their contribution to a cumulative process of development, and the means of implementing selectivity might be illuminating both for national and for collective efforts in the future.

Second, the relative roles of the market and of the state merit continuing attention in LDCs. What are the criteria for defining the sphere of action of each, and the most effective forms of intervention (direct or indirect) to be adopted by the state? It is undeniable both that, beyond ideological options, technical elements do enter into play, and that, under the guise of technical "purity", orthodox theory harbours a sizeable ideological content. More policy-oriented research on different combinations of market and state action in the areas of technology, capital markets, export promotion, relations with TNCs, and the influence of the degrees of development and administrative capacity on their effects, might be built on the considerable relevant research undertaken in the last two decades on these issues. In broad terms, theoretical and empirical progress in these areas has scarcely been integrated at all with the literature of international economics or that of CSR. Two specific questions relating to the role of market and state intervention in CSR planning might be mentioned: (i) the trade policies most suited to the implementation of joint production agreements, and the appropriate criteria for designing margins of preference, and (ii) the analysis of decisions that must be adopted by multinational authorities or multinational economic units, in different categories of countries, markets and commodities.

Third, in LDCs with limited capital markets, narrow horizons, dynamic external economies, and diffuse comparative advantages, it is difficult for national private firms — except perhaps when their control becomes highly concentrated in economic groups — to play the leading role in industrial development. Consequently, in the absence of public enterprises, the role remains vacant or is taken on by TNCs. Thus, the anti-state bias that characterizes the conventional literature tends to limit the possibilities for dynamic and autonomous development. More research effort is merited on the mechanisms and norms for public enterprises which assure their efficient functioning. What direct and indirect norms may be established to improve their contribution to industrial development? How can their decisions be better subjected to norms of social efficiency, in the sense that they satisfy the specific objectives for which they were created, and the general objectives of national and CSR development strategy (Sheahan 1976). The literature on criteria and mechanisms for the regulation of public enterprises in LDCs and on the experience of specific cases is particularly scanty.

Notes

1 An excellent critical survey of the approach appears in Whitman (1975).
2 A study by ECIEL, for example, which covers 14 products of the Latin American manufacturing sector, shows that in those cases where the availability of resources and the transport costs are not determining factors, the comparative advantages of numerous products may be shifted from one country to another by means of slight variations in exchange rates. See Carnoy (1970) and Grunwald (1976).
3 This regulation must prevent cost-reduction effects from turning into "foreign-profit creation". See Tironi (1977).

4 This refers to those decisions centralized in an agency, whether supranational or multinational, with authority over agencies in each individual country. Other decisions should be centralized at the level of national governments. Three decision-making levels are thus being distinguished. A more extensive analysis, within this framework of ideas can be found in Ffrench-Davis (1974).

5 General analyses are to be gound in Hirschman (1958, ch. 10), Chenery (1959). Brief references to polarization in customs unions can be found in Robson (1971), Introduction), UNCTAD (1973), and Wionczek (1966, Introduction). On the role of information, an analysis that is very relevant to this subject is to be found in Arrow (1974).

6 Deciding the geographical location can also improve the bargaining position of member countries as a whole *vis-à-vis* TNCs. In fact, the assigned country can enjoy the power derived from the sum of the partners' markets.

7 A somewhat similar discussion is to be found in UNECAFE (1973) and Kamsu (1976). An alternative, which is found in the field of partial integration agreements, puts forward the allocation of activities on the basis of ''comparative costs'' and the subsequent redistribution of the financial benefits within the enterprise. If this is to be done, it is stipulated that all common market countries should participate in the ownership of the enterprise or in the surplus which it generates, according to the size of the market which each provides. See Little (1966). This latter proposition may be used in conjunction with the planning of regional investments, in order to reduce the danger of polarization of productive activities.

8 See Salgado (1974). An analysis of the first programme approved by the Andean countries, in the basic metals and machinery sectors, including a discussion of some of the problems faced in its design and implementation appears in Gana (1976). See also JUNAC (1980). By 1979, there were also programmes in the petrochemical and transport equipment sectors.

9 The Andean countries adopted a system of this nature. The scheme consists in the joint programming of the new economic activities oriented towards the regional market, and, for this reason, each country is assigned the right to develop certain industrial complexes without competition from the other members. They must, however, face that of third countries though protected by the CET. It is, therefore, a mixed mechanism, which centralizes decisions as to what and where to produce and decentralizes numerous decisions as to how, how much and when to produce. See Ffrench-Davis (1977).

10 To the extent that the level and the structure of the CET are intended to correct market distortions which are common to, and of the same magnitude in, all countries, such a subsidy will be unjustifiable. If, however, the distortions differ from country to country and are more intense for the product in question in the country assigned (for example, a labour-intensive product in a country suffering from an unemployment problem larger than that of other member countries), a certain level of subsidy would be justified on second-best policy grounds; higher levels would be inefficient for the region.

References

Arrow, K. 1974. "Limited knowledge and economic analysis", *American Economic Review,* March, pp. 1—10.

Carnoy, M. 1970. "A welfare analysis of Latin American economic unions: six industry studies", *Journal of Political Economy,* pp. 626—54.

Chenery, H. 1959. "The interdependence of investment decisions", in M. Abramovitz, *et al., The Allocation of Economic Resources,* Stanford University Press.

Corden, M. 1972. "Economies of scale and custom union theory", *Journal of Political Economy,* June.

Corea, G. 1977. *New Directions and New Structures for Trade and Development,* Report by the Secretary General to UNCTAD, IV, UN. TD/183/Rev. 1.

Dell, S. 1963. *Trade Blocks and Common Markets,* Constable.

Diaz-Alejandro, C. 1973. "The Andean Common Market: gestation and outlook", in R. Eckaus & P. Rosenstein-Rodan (eds.), *Analysis of Development Problems,* North-Holland.

Ffrench-Davis, R. 1974. "Planificacion en el Pacto Andino y el Arancel Externo Comun", *Revista de la Integracion,* N°17, INTAL, Buenos Aires, September, pp. 87—104.

Ffrench-Davis, R. 1977. "The Andean Pact: a model of economic integration for developing countries", in J. Grunwald (ed.), *Latin America in a Changing World,* Sage Publications, and in *World Development,* January-February.

Ffrench-Davis, R. 1979. *Economia Internacional: teorias y politicas para el desarrollo,* Fondo de Cultura Economica.

Fortin, C. 1978. "Third World commodity policy at the crossroads: some fundamental issues", *IFDA Dossier* 15, January-February.

Frenkel, J. & Johnson, H. (eds.), 1976. *The Monetary Approach to the Balance of Payments,* Allen & Unwin, London.

Gana, E. 1976. "La programacion metalmecanica del Acuerdo de Cartagena y las empresas transnacionales", CEPAL/DIDE/ET/164, December.

Ghai, D. 1974. "State trading and regional economic integration, the East African experience", *Journal of Common Market Studies,* 12, pp. 296—318.

Ghai, D. 1976. "Comments on integration of less developed areas", in Machlup (ed.), see below.

Grunwald, J. 1976. "Industrializacion e integracion economica de America Latina", *Revista de Economia Latinoamericana,* Caracas.

Helleiner, G. 1978. "World market imperfections and developing countries", *ODC,* May.

Hirschman, A. 1958. *The Strategy of Economic Development,* Yale University Press.

Johnson, H. 1976. "The monetary approach to the balance of payments", in Frenkel & Johnson (eds.), see above.

JUNAC 1980. "Informacion sobre el Programa Sectorial de Desarrollo de la Industria Metalmecanica", JUN/di462/Rev. 1, June.

Kamsu, R. 1976. "Comments on Integration of less developed areas", in Machlup (ed.), see below.

Lipsey, R. 1976. "Comments on types of economic integration", in Machlup (ed.), see below.

Little, I. 1966. "Regional international companies as an approach to economic integration", *Journal of Common Market Studies,* December, pp. 180—86. Reproduced in Robson (ed.), see below.

Lizano, F. 1976. "Integration of less developed areas on different levels of development", in Machlup (ed.), see below.

Machlup, F. (ed.), 1976. *Economic Integration: Worldwide, Regional, Sectoral.* International Economic Association, The Macmillan Press Ltd.

Myrdal, G. 1957. *Economic Theory and Underdeveloped Regions,* London, Duckworth.

Robson, P. (ed.), 1971. *International Economic Integration,* Penguin Readings.

Salgado, G. 1974. "La Integracion economica de paises en desarrollo y la funcion de una planificacion industrial conjunta", Development Planning Committee, United Nations.

Sheahan, J. 1976. "Public enterprise in developing countries", in W. Shepard (ed.), *Public Enterprise,* Lexington Books, Mass.

Stewart, F. 1981. "Industrialization, technical change and the international division of labour", this volume, chapter 5.

Tironi, E. 1977. "Customs union theory in the presence of foreign firms", mimeo, CIEPLAN.

UNCTAD 1973. "The distribution of costs and benefits in economic integration among developing countries", *Current Problems of Economic Integration,* TD/P/394, United Nations.

UNCTAD 1975. "El problema de la distribucion de beneficios y costos, y medidas correctivas seleccionadas", *Problemas Actuales de la Integracion,* TD/R/517, United Nations.

UNECAFE 1973. *Asian Industrial survey for regional cooperation,* United Nations.

Vaitsos, C. 1974. *Intercountry Income Distribution and Transnational Enterprises,* Clarendon Press, Oxford.

Vaitsos, C. 1978. "Crisis in regional economic cooperation (integration) among developing countries", *World Development.*

Westphal, L. 1980. "The infant industry argument and the relation of trade policy to industrial strategy", in M. Syrgvin & S. Teitel (eds.), *Trade, stability, technology, and equity in Latin America,* Academic Press, forthcoming.

Whitman, M. 1975. "Global monetarism and the monetary approach to the balance of payments", *Brookings Papers on Economic Activity,* N°3.

Wionczek, M. 1966. "Integracion economica y distribucion regional de actividades industriales; estudio comparativo de las experiencias de Centro-America y el Africa Oriental", *El Trimestre Economico,* N°131, July-September.

Part III

International Finance
in Theory and Practice

Chapter 7

The Economics of IMF Conditionality

John Williamson*

Introduction

One of the purposes for which the International Monetary Fund was created is that of providing balance-of-payments assistance to members suffering temporary deficits. After a slow start, in which its activities were confined almost exclusively to Latin America as a result of the pre-emption of European problems by the Marshall Plan, IMF lending became significant in the second half of the 1950s. By then the Fund had already established its "tranche" policy, under which the first tranche (25% of quota) was available on demand, and the second tranche (the first credit tranche) subject to minimal conditions, while the subsequent three tranches were made available only after a country had agreed with the Fund a program deemed adequate to secure payments adjustment.

Subsequent developments have preserved this basic distinction between "low-conditionality" and "high-conditionality" Fund facilities. The low-conditionality facilities have been augmented by the Compensatory Financing Facility, to enable primary-producing members suffering an export shortfall to draw up to the amount of the estimated shortfall; the Buffer Stock Facility, to help provide finance for members' contributions to approved buffer stock schemes; and (temporarily, in 1974—6) the Oil Facility, which provided finance for up to a specified proportion of members' "oil deficits".[1] All three low-conditionality facilities are subject to limits related to the size of a member's quota, and also require an undertaking that the country will endeavour to find appropriate solutions to any payments difficulties it may have. Meanwhile the high-conditionality facilities have been extended only by the addition in 1974 of the Extended Facility, intended to provide finance in larger quantities and for longer periods to members whose adjustment is judged to require structural change and not just financial stabilization, and which agree

* The author is indebted to members of the Seminar for comments that have resulted in a number of changes.

121

on a program to that effect with the Fund. Something like 90 per cent of Fund lending was made under the low-conditionality facilities in the years up to 1979, but the second oil shock seems to have brought a revival of borrowing from the high-conditionality facilities, the sums for which have been augmented by the Supplementary Financing ("Witteveen") Facility.

The above factual summary about the Fund's conditional lending suggests two sets of questions relevant to this volume. First, what is the logic for having both low-conditionality and high-conditionality facilities, and is the present balance between the two appropriate in the light of that logic? Second, what sort of economic theory underlies Fund policies regarding drawings from the high-conditionality facilities, and do those policies react to the disadvantage of developing countries? The remainder of this paper is devoted to suggesting answers to those questions.

The logic of conditionality

Fund credit has always been provided on terms that are to some extent concessional (although the margin of concessionality has shrunk in recent years as a result of the attempt to make the SDR a more competitive reserve asset). Were it not so, indeed, countries would have no motivation to borrow from the Fund. There are some economists (e.g., Vaubel 1980) who conclude from this that the Fund has no business existing, since that very existence creates a problem of moral hazard. (Provision of balance-of-payments finance on concessional terms gives an incentive to countries to qualify for this assistance, which they can do by inflating and so creating a payments deficit that will qualify for the concessional assistance.) And even those who might be prepared to brush that viewpoint aside must recognize that the provision of finance on concessional terms inevitably requires the operation of some rationing mechanism to restrict demand to no more than the available supply.

In the case of the low-conditionality facilities, the principal safeguard-against-moral-hazard *cum* rationing mechanism is provided by the specification of objective circumstances *beyond a country's own control* which, if they create a deficit, qualify the country for access to Fund finance. This is most clearly manifest in the Compensatory Financing Facility, while the Oil Facility and the Buffer Stock Facility also fit this category reasonably well. Only the first credit tranche[2] fails to fit. In essence, what the Fund does in the typical low-conditionality facility is to provide insurance against a class of risks which do not seem well suited to insurance by a private market (and which have certainly not in the past been insurable in any existing market). Provided that access to finance can be effectively limited to countries that are suffering objectively-specifiable deficits due to circumstances that really are outside their control, credit will indeed be rationed and there will be no problem of moral hazard, while the countries receiving the insurance will presumably benefit, even if this insurance scheme did not receive a subsidy from non-members. (In fact, there is such a subsidy element, though it is not large.)

The logic of the high-conditionality facilities is quite different. They are intended to aid the recovery of countries that forfeit their credit-worthiness, often as the result of misgovernment. In general, a set of policy reforms adequate to restore a country's situation in the medium term should not be expected to eliminate its current account deficit immediately, since the cost of abrupt adjustment is typically very high. (One of the best-documented facts about the balance of payments is that long-run elasticities are typically much higher than short-run elasticities.) The question is whether bankers could be expected to lend (on other than penal terms) in order to tide countries over that difficult gap before visible evidence of recovery appears. Presumably, even if they were so willing, they would require assurance, such as is provided by acceptance of an IMF standby, that policies really have changed and that the new policies will be maintained long enough to secure adjustment. However, the one attempt to date of the banks to negotiate macro policy changes with a government (Peru) was not a success. I suspect this was not an accident, but the result of the fact that commercial banks are inherently unsuited to the role of negotiating policies with sovereign governments — partly because they are at an informational disadvantage as compared to the IMF, partly because optimal competitive strategies for individual banks may not add up to coherent pressure for rational policies, and partly because neither commercial banks nor the governments of their home countries seem likely to be able to play the role of the foreign ''bogeyman'' who can be blamed for unpopular policy changes, at least not without a dangerous fanning of nationalistic flames.

Whether the IMF need itself provide credit, and whether in that case the credit should not carry a commercial interest rate, is more debatable. There do, however, seem to be advantages in the institution that negotiates the policy changes being in a position to put up a fair bit of money directly, rather than simply giving a seal of approval that with luck will induce the private market to resume lending. And perhaps there is something to be said for a small act of solidarity by the international community to a country that has set about reform after a period of gross misgovernment, instead of magnifying the problems faced by the reforming administration, as occurs when loans are available only at interest rates that reflect the problems inherited from the past. The Fund's conditions no doubt need to be tough enough to avoid the problem of moral hazard.

There therefore seems to me to be a basic logic to the broad structure of Fund lending policies. But that is not to say that there is no scope for rationalization and extension. Regarding low-conditionality lending, the following questions are worth consideration.

(1) Can one justify the anachronism of low-conditionality lending in the first credit tranche?

(2) Why should shortfalls in the value of primary product exports be the only shock due to circumstances beyond a country's own control for which low-conditionality finance is available? Are payments deficits caused by the need to import food because of crop failures, or because of increased food prices, less deserving of finance?[3] Or payments deficits caused by a reduction in the market for manufactured exports? Should not any temporary deficit caused by factors outside a country's own control qualify a country for low-conditionality finance (as urged in UNDP/UNCTAD 1979)? What about a deficit due to an increased oil price? Don't we also wish to help the permanently-impacted to adjust? Should not low-conditionality finance also be available for a *tapering* proportion of any *permanent* adverse change due to factors outside a country's own control?

(3) Is there any scope for extending this principle to cover capital inflows? In an age when over 50 per cent of the foreign exchange receipts of some developing countries consist of capital inflows and comparable sums are involved in debt-service payments, any interruption to lending inevitably creates an impossible payments problem. Can one rely on the banks not to interrupt the flow of lending for arbitrary reasons? Could the Fund help the banks to design rational lending strategies and avoid over-exposure by agreeing with its members a set of mutually-consistent current balance targets (which would of course need to be published)? Might it not also be desirable to secure a major funding of LDC debt in order to reduce exposure to the risk of interruptions in the flow of lending (most of which is needed simply to roll over old debt)?

High-conditionality terms

However much the low-conditionality facilities are extended, it is surely right that access to them should be restricted to occasions when deficits are due to circumstances beyond a country's control. But deficits also arise from a country's own actions — principally as a result of the pursuit of over-expansionary demand policies. As argued above, the purpose of the high-conditionality facilities is to help countries that reach the end of the road to make a new start without imposing impossible short-term hardship. The question that arises is whether the terms the Fund imposes are appropriate to achieving the desired end, namely payments adjustment, without causing unnecessary immediate suffering.

Fund terms are based on mainstream balance-of-payments theory. In my view this is not a particularly controversial area of economics: by now it is well understood that the various "approaches" that generated such controversy in the past are best viewed as complementary components of a general equilibrium model. While there is no single specification of such a model which would command general assent, there are a series of propositions that come out of just about every reasonable specification. Let me list some of the obvious and important ones:

(1) that the current balance varies positively with world income and negatively with domestic absorption;

(2) that the division of (both world and national) expenditure between domestically-produced goods and foreign-produced goods varies positively with the real exchange rate;[4]

(3) that (2), plus the fact *(sic)* that the Marshall-Lerner condition is invariably satisfied in the medium run, implies that (after an adjustment period) the current balance varies positively with the real exchange rate;

(4) that the division of (primarily national) expenditure between domestically-produced and foreign-produced goods can also be influenced by an endless variety of controls and restrictions;

(5) that at given nominal exchange rates there is an equilibrium distribution of money in the world economy, hence additional domestic credit expansion (DCE) will ultimately *all* leak out abroad (with a fixed exchange rate and given controls).

How far do such generally accepted propositions suffice to take one toward endorsing the characteristic features of Fund programs? First and foremost, there is absolutely no doubt that monetary factors play a major role in determining payments outcomes; one can perfectly well recognize this without suffering from a monetarist compulsion to organize one's thoughts around the money market. It follows that any plausible program for payments adjustment must provide for an appropriate ceiling on domestic credit expansion. The approach used in the Fund to calculate acceptable ceilings is described as "financial programming" and has been sketched by Robichek (1967), but the formulae are not really all that revealing.

Second, there is usually (though not inevitably) a strong case for accompanying monetary restraint by fiscal restraint. The fundamental reason for this is that bank credit to the private sector typically (and this is especially true in countries without highly developed capital markets) plays a strategic role in financing the purchase of intermediate goods by the tradable-goods-producing sectors — exactly the sectors whose output needs to be maintained or preferably expanded in the interests of payments adjustment. A curtailment in total credit expansion without a reduction in the government deficit inevitably throws the whole burden of credit restriction on the private sector, and thereby threatens the supply of tradable goods and thus the recovery of the balance of payments.

However, both monetary restraint and fiscal restraint constitute expenditure-reducing methods of improving the balance of payments. Whenever over-expansionary policies have been pursued for long enough to generate an inflation that undermined the competitiveness of domestically-produced tradable goods, expenditure reduction alone cannot restore internal and external balance simultaneously. For that purpose it is also necessary to introduce an expenditure-switching policy: devaluation is that invariably preferred by the Fund.

The Fund's preference for devaluation rather than intensification of trade and payments restrictions derives from the general presumption stemming from "orthodox" economic theory that the least-cost way of satisfying a budget constraint is to let the market decide how it is to be done, except where there are specific reasons for believing that there are divergences between private and social costs and benefits. This is a presumption that I share, though I am perhaps more inclined than the average economist to stress the importance of avoiding a forced pace of adjustment. I suppose that my discomfort with the orthodox presumption in the face of peremptory (or, even worse, oscillating) adjustment requirements stems less from any rigorous demonstration of the superiority of controls than from a feeling that all bets are then off, perhaps coupled with the observation that in the past governments have often felt driven to the adoption of controls in such circumstances.

Another point that merits mention concerns the logic of the Fund practice of placing limits on short-term and medium-term foreign borrowing. These limits at first sight seem paradoxical, inasmuch as they restrict the extent to which a country may improve its balance of payments through capital inflows, despite the fact that the object of the exercise is precisely that of improving its balance of payments. To the extent that any *sustained* payments improvement requires *current account* adjustment, however, such limits may be considered rational, since current account adjustment — and indeed financial stabilization — can be undermined by capital inflows prompted by the restoration of confidence (the "Southern Cone Problem", vide Diaz-Alejandro, 1981). Presumably a committed believer in rational expectations would argue that this cannot occur, since the market would forsee the implications of its actions and thus refrain from making loans so large as to undermine the stabilization program that was the attraction in the first place. The same logic would, however, seem to question whether countries can ever borrow to the point of undermining their own credit-worthiness, while the Fund as an institution very much in touch with reality knows that they sometimes can and do.

Endorsement of the broad principles of Fund conditionality does not imply a judgement that the conditions imposed by the Fund have always been well conceived. I list below the types of criticism of past Fund practice that I think probably have a substantial element of validity.

(i) Insufficient recognition that devaluation not only has expenditure-switching, thus demand-expansionary, effects, but also absorption-reducing effects (Dornbusch 1973, Krugman & Taylor 1978). This has led to "overkill" in contractionary policies especially where — as probably in most non-NIC LDCs, on account of low substitution elasticities on the supply side — the absorption-reducing effects outweigh the expenditure-switching effects on demand.

(ii) A somewhat cavalier attitude to the income-redistributive consequences of adjustment programs. It can hardly be doubted that the major price changes involved in large devaluations (especially when accompanied by liberalization) have major effects on the incomes of specific groups. But two central points must be recognized. First, the process of income redistribution is an integral part of the mechanism

127

by which adjustment takes place — by which resources are redeployed and absorption is curtailed. To wipe out the redistributive consequences of devaluation would inevitably neutralize the effects one was seeking in the first place. Second, redistribution is not necessarily regressive: that is an empirical question on which it seems doubtful whether any striking generalizations are possible (Johnson & Salop 1980). Indeed, the Heckscher-Ohlin theorem suggests that devaluation-*cum*-liberalization is likely to redistribute income toward the abundant factor, namely unskilled labour in most LDCs, and thus have progressive distributional consequences. (That will not make it any more popular with urban self-styled radicals who retain a realistic sense of self interest.) My own inclination is to believe that, while the Fund could profitably be more self-conscious than it has been in the past about the distributional consequences of the programs it is sponsoring, there are strict limits to the extent to which it will be possible to minimize the pain of the losers without jeopardizing the success of the program.

(iii) A preference for large and sudden devaluations to a new "fixed" rate, rather than for gradual (crawling) devaluations designed to maintain the real exchange rate in the vicinity of what is believed to be an equilibrium rate. Since a supposedly once-for-all devaluation has to make allowance for the inflation that will be induced by the devaluation itself, it is necessary to overdo the initial change. This creates three unnecessary problems. First, it creates a need to perform inherently-speculative calculations regarding the extent of the inflation that will be provoked by the devaluation, in order to pick the new nominal peg. Second, the implied changes in the real exchange rate before equilibrium is achieved will produce temporary allocative distortions and income redistribution which serve no social purpose. (Moreover, if the real rate implied by the new peg is not credible in the medium term, the devaluation may fail to induce the allocative changes that are desired.) Third, it will worsen the capital inflow problem alluded to above and so intensify problems of monetary control.

(iv) An attempt to compress adjustment into too short a time scale. The very logic of having the Fund impose conditions rather than letting the country act convincingly first and then go to the private banks is to allow adjustment to be spread out over time. And, except in the easy case where adjustment requires no more than the elimination of excess demand, it surely is true that precipitate adjustment is costly adjustment. Yet Fund programs have typically aimed at a payments turnround within a year, that being the period for which standby programs in the higher credit tranches have normally applied, and for which countries have therefore remained subject to close Fund monitoring. It is true that there have recently been important changes: the Extended Facility involves conditions over a three-year period, and even standbys have increasingly been granted for periods of longer than a year. It seems to me that there is a very stong case for welcoming these innovations and encouraging the Fund to take an even longer time perspective in designing stabilization-*cum*-adjustment programs. But this has one or possibly two corollaries. First, it is necessary to extend the period for which Fund conditionality applies, which is presumably unwelcome to at least some of the critics of conditionality. Second, it raises the question as to what happens when a country faithfully complies with the conditions imposed, but still does not experience a recovery in its balance of payments, perhaps because of a sequence of unfavourable shocks. Is it really right to impose ever more onerous conditions, until either the balance of payments recovers or a social revolution is ignited? Is there not a case for creating some international mechanism that could bail out the occasional hard case of this type? Might that provide a more logical and socially constructive role for the Trust Fund than providing interest subsidies?

Concluding remarks

If one regards the hallmarks of "accepted Western economic theory" as recognition that budget constraints exist and ultimately have to be respected, and that there is a general presumption that the least-cost way of satisfying them is to let the market mechanism operate except where there are specific reasons for doing otherwise, then there is no escaping classification of the Fund as a conventional Western economic institution and the author as a conventional Western economist. As readers may have detected, I have little sympathy for that type of "radical" critique which interprets liberalization policies as an attempt by the capitalist West to use the Fund to foist policies on LDCs which benefit the former at the expense of the latter. I regard the serious questions about Fund policies as neither such general conspiratorial allegations, nor the appropriateness of the mainstream eclectic theoretical framework employed by the Fund, but more mundane questions — above all of the time horizon within which Fund programs are designed to achieve their results. In urging that the Fund take a longer view, however, one should not encourage it to water down conditionality to the point where acceptance of a Fund standby no longer provides reasonable assurance that a payments turnround will in fact be achieved — that would simply destroy the Fund's ability to restore a member's credit-worthiness with the private market. Rather, the aims should be to limit high conditionality to countries that have come to require it by dint of their own past mismanagement, to allow countries in this state to choose the least-cost path to re-establishment of their credit-worthiness while ensuring that that re-establishment turns out to be merited by the subsequent course of events, and perhaps providing some back-up facility for the odd case where the country conscientiously pursues appropriate policies but is afflicted by a succession of misfortunes.

Notes

1 The Fund has also added the SDR scheme, to provide unconditional liquidity, and, outside of its regular resources (financed principally by gold sales), the Trust Fund, to provide highly-concessional loans to low-income members.

2 The tranche "before" the first credit tranche (which used to be called the gold tranche and is now known as the reserve tranche) results from the member contributing reserves to the Fund, and thus does not raise the same issues as the Fund's other conditional facilities.

3 It was announced during the 1980 Annual Meetings that the Fund is actively studying a mechanism to provide financing in such situations; see IMF (1980).

4 I depart from my past practice and define the exchange rate as the domestic currency price of foreign exchange.

References

Díaz-Alejandro, C. 1981. "Southern Cone Stabilization Plans", in W.R. Cline & S. Weintraub (eds.), *Economic Stabilization in Developing Countries,* Brookings Institution.

Dornbusch, R. 1973. "Devaluation, Money, and Nontraded Goods", *American Economic Review,* December.

IMF *Survey,* October 13, 1980.

Johnson, O. & Salop, J. 1980. "Distributional Aspects of Stabilization Programs in Developing Countries", *IMF Staff Papers,* March.

Krugman, P. & Taylor, L. 1978. "Contractionary Effects of Devaluation", *Journal of International Economics,* August.

Robichek, E.W. 1967. "Financial Programming Exercises of the IMF in Latin America", address to a seminar of Brazilian professors, Rio de Janeiro, September 1967.

UNDP/UNCTAD 1979. *The Balance of Payments Adjustment Process in Developing Countries: A Report to the Group of 24,* United Nations.

Vaubel, R. 1980. "The Return to the New European Monetary System: Objectives, Incentives, Perspectives", *Carnegie-Rochester Conference Series on Public Policy,* Autumn 1980.

Chapter 8

Tropical Reflections on the History and Theory of International Financial Markets

Edmar Lisboa Bacha and *Carlos F. Díaz-Alejandro*

Private international financial intermediation has witnessed successive cycles for the last 160 years. In this century, it blossomed before the first World War and through the 1920s. In the 1930s and 1940s, private capital markets went into an eclipse, to reappear prudently in the 1950s, booming in the 1960s and 1970s. Theorizing about financial markets has on the whole followed those cycles. Few are the examples of powerful propositions emerging from general financial theories which are independent of historically specific institutional arrangements.

This paper discusses the interplay of financial aspects of the history of world capitalism with theorizing about financial markets, carried out mainly in "Northern" countries. It is organized as follows. Three "epochs" in financial arrangements and theories are first reviewed, with special emphasis on their impact on peripheral countries. They are the pre-1929 years, 1944—1973, and 1973—1980. Then some systemic issues of international financial arrangements for the 1980s are discussed. Finally, analytical and empirical problems suggested by unexpected consequences of recent attempts at financial reform in Latin America are debated.

Frequent references will be made to "orthodoxy". This term is not easy to define; it may be helpful to separate "academic" from "practical" orthodoxy. The former is the product of leading academic centers of the time; it tends to be flexible and agnostic. Its leading thinkers often are its own major critics, frequently curious about heterodox notions. "Practical orthodoxy" is more assertive. It is found in the editorials of the business press, among private or public executives with Masters' degrees, and among the more politically or financially ambitious academics. The latter sometimes play a double role: in their Northern universities, disciplined by their colleagues, they are cautious scientists; during their summer tours of the periphery, their *libido imperante* unleashed, they become fountain-heads of practical orthodoxy.

It is the practical orthodoxy that puts the system to work and typically sets the Northern tone in North-South debates. As such it will be the main focus of our analysis.

The Pax Britannica

The pre-1929 international financial order enjoyed a degree of intellectual hegemony which has never been regained. The gold-exchange standard was regarded as the natural regulator of the balance of payments. Current account deficits and increases in international reserves were financed by using bonds with long maturities and fixed interest rates as well as via direct investments. Under the long *Pax Britannica* some countries (Germany, the USA) graduated from the role of capital importers to that of capital exporters. At least until the 1920s, London ruled the waves and regulated the whole system, whose occasional crises were regarded as passing aberrations or a necessary purging of excesses.

National financial systems showed greater heterogeneity. In the United States, populist pressures blocked the creation of a central bank until early in this century. France and Germany developed financial systems more centralized and state-dominated than that of the United Kingdom, as analyzed by Alexander Gershenkron. Apparently, British hegemony in international relations of all types explains the relative homogeneity of the international financial rules of the game, in contrast with those applicable nationally.

African and Asian colonies had little choice in their financial systems, and tended to follow prevailing orthodoxy. Several independent Latin American countries, however, had difficulties in adhering faithfully to the gold-exchange standard.[1] Mexico followed a silver standard for many years, while silver depreciated *vis-à-vis* gold. Argentina and Brazil often resorted to an inconvertible paper standard, frequently accompanied by fiscal deficits and inflation. (The USA went through a similar period after its Civil War.)

These Latin American experiments with flexible exchange rates were viewed with fascinated disgust by orthodox scholars and bankers. The recurrent need for foreign finance as well as domestic political pressures would sporadically dictate a return to the gold-exchange standard and greater controls over domestic credit expansion.

134

Foreign missions played important roles in attempted returns to orthodoxy. Examples include the Montagu Mission to Brazil in 1924 and those of Professor Krammer to several Andean countries.[2] At least in the case of the Brazilian return to the gold-exchange standard in the 1920s, the economic results are generally regarded as negative. (During the 1920s the League of Nations also participated in missions associated with "Stabilization Plans", particularly within Europe.)

The conditionality attached to international lending before 1929 included not only that linked to the natural desire of bankers to be punctually paid at least the interest due on loans. Political considerations also played a role in regulating access to capital markets. French and German lending were heavily influenced by political factors, as illustrated by the former's loans to Czarist Russia and the latter's loan to the Middle East.[3] Brazilian access to the New York market was blocked by Herbert Hoover, then Secretary of Commerce, in retaliation for the Brazilian coffee valorization scheme; Brazilian access to the London market in the late 1920s was also discreetly vetoed by the Foreign Office in retaliation for the Brazilian withdrawal from the League of Nations.[4] The conditionality imposed before 1929 on the weakest peripheral countries included foreign control over their tariff revenues and other aspects of their fiscal and monetary machinery; this was the case in some Caribbean and Central American nations, in a fashion similar to that of Zaire during the 1970s.

The great depression of the 1930s destroyed the gold-exchange standard and international capital markets as they existed before 1929. The prestige of high finance collapsed; in the USA, financiers were the target of New Deal attacks, and new legislation limited the flexibility of national and international financial intermediaries. European nazism/fascism popularized exchange and financial controls going beyond those practiced in other industrialized countries. Several industrial countries declared moratoria of domestic debts and witnessed drastic restructuring of their financial systems.

Peripheral countries with certain political autonomy, such as Argentina, Brazil and Colombia, reacted to the Great Depression with a fairly rapid abandonment of gold standard orthodoxy, wisely avoiding classical advice. Thus, Brazil was advised by a mission headed by Sir Otto Niemeyer, of the Bank of England, to return to a fixed exchange rate and to maintain convertibility, *in July 1931!*[5] These large or active Latin American countries allowed substantial depreciations of their exchange rate, imposed exchange controls, and maintained a reasonable degree of domestic liquidity. Normal debt

135

servicing was suspended in most cases. Partly because of the closing of international capital markets, Latin American countries showed greater interest in mobilizing domestic resources via the tax system and the creation of new government controlled credit institutions. The economic performance of these countries during the 1930s was remarkably good, better than that of major industrialized countries.

The Pax Americana

The international financial order that emerged from Bretton Woods in 1944, lasting until 1973, initially reflected the 1930s disenchantment with *laissez faire* in financial transactions and was influenced by Fabian/New Deal notions then dominant in the United Kingdom and the United States. The International Monetary Fund (IMF) was born, accepting changes in exchange rates to correct "fundamental disequilibrium" and allowing controls over capital movements. The creation of the International Bank for Reconstruction and Development (IBRD) reflected pessimism regarding the viability of private financial intermediation in the postwar world. In the USA, the official EXIMBANK, created in the 1930s originally to finance trade with the USSR, was to play an important role in financing US exports of capital goods, and was a critical institution in US-Latin American economic relations. Already in the 1950s and even more so in the 1960s, the orginal Fabian/New Deal flavour of the Bretton Woods institutions was diluted, but they continued to reflect a degree of theoretical and practical eclecticism absent in the pre-1929 international financial order.

At least during the late 1940s and 1950s, both national and international financial intermediation received low priority. The ultra-Keynesian notion that "money does not matter" could easily be extended to "financial intermediation does not matter". It was not until the late 1950s that Europe abandoned rigorous exchange controls. (The United Kingdom maintained them until 1979!)

Early in the postwar period, a new practical orthodoxy appeared regarding capital movements. Especially in the USA, it became common to hear advice aimed at peripheral countries regarding the importance of maintaining a favorable climate for direct foreign investments from the North. Direct foreign investment, supplier's credits, and official development assistance of various sorts made up the bulk of capital inflows into the periphery well into the 1960s. All of these forms of finance implied a complex and fairly intimate relationship between lenders and borrowers.

Academic orthodoxy had surprisingly little to say about the benefits and costs of the postwar structure of capital flows between North and South. There was a tendency to add up all forms of capital flows into one aggregate necessary to finance the "foreign exchange gap". A common attitude was that the greater this aggregate flow, the better all around. This academic complacency was first punctured by peripheral (and Australian, Canadian, and European) criticism of some of the consequences of direct foreign investment and of multinational corporations. Some aspects of official development assistance also came under closer scrutiny, leading to more sophisticated evaluations of the grant element involved in such flows.

As noted earlier, already in the 1950s the IMF and the IBRD began to depart from the vision of at least some of their founding fathers, especially that of John Maynard Keynes. The IBRD stuck to the financing of specific projects, avoiding program lending. The IBRD also refused to lend to oil state enterprises, arguing that there were plenty of private oil corporations willing to invest. The IMF staff increasingly favored fixed exchange rates buttressed by rigorous credit policies, in a pattern similar to the pre-1929 rules of the game. In its dealings with peripheral countries given to heterodoxy, such as several Latin American countries, the IMF missions revived the spirit of Montagu and Niemeyer, advocating stiff stabilization plans. It could be argued that at least during the 1950s the leverage of the IMF missions was not smaller than those of Montagu and Niemeyer, as international credit sources in the 1950s were few, and tended to follow the leadership of the IMF (and the US Treasury). The consequences of the practical orthodoxy of the IMF were not very different from those of the Montagu mission.

As late as the 1960s, those advocating greater resource transfers from North to South would call for more official development assistance under various forms. Regional development banks were created, adding new official financial intermediaries. New aid relationships were sought. Hopes were also expressed for a new spirit in direct foreign investment.

In the meantime, the great postwar economic expansion which culminated in the early 1970s was creating new conditions eroding the postwar practical orthodoxy. Almost accidentally, a truly international capital market emerged in the mid-1960s, in the form of Eurocurrency credits. Growing macroeconomic disharmonies among the industrialized countries in the late 1960s, the US involvement in Vietnam, and increased capital mobility put enormous pressures on fixed parities. These circumstances led to abandonment by the US of gold convertibility in August 1971 and to generalized floating of key currencies in early 1973. This *Annus Mirabilis* culminated with the sharp rise in oil prices, putting an end to the postwar era of cheap energy.

Pax Arabica?

The period 1973—1980 has been highly unusual in the history of international finance. A new type of capital exporter has emerged, which has no historical precedent. Consider the following contrast between OPEC capital exporters and those of earlier eras:

a) The military power of major OPEC countries is trivial, certainly insufficient to enforce financial contracts against recalcitrant debtors. It has been noted that every lender ultimately needs bailiffs at his back;[6] OPEC does not have them.

b) OPEC countries lack capital goods industries, or indeed an extensive industrial base, to achieve the real transfer ultimately desired by capital importers. Their technological base is weak. It is difficult to imagine the equivalent to British exports of railway equipment or US direct foreign investment for the OPEC case.

c) OPEC capital exporters had only limited financial institutions of their own; they relied heavily on financial intermediaries of industrialized countries.

d) OPEC national currencies are used only marginally as reserve or vehicle currencies; the influence of OPEC over international monetary arrangements is growing, but it is still modest.

e) The major component of OPEC wealth is a non-renewable resource. If investments in financial or real assets yield low rates of return, OPEC countries will tend to adjust by decreasing their oil output, i.e., by investing in oil underground. Thus, part of OPEC's "home investment" can *decrease* the world's aggregate supply in the short and medium term.

These considerations imply a good deal of interdependence between the old and the new capital exporteres, involving both economic and political aspects. The latter have become highly visible since 1973, in contrast with previous years, when they were discreetly hidden. The network of trade flows has also become more complex and multilateral, involving greater "triangularity" among old and new capital exporters and the Third World.

The Eurocurrency market, already vigorous before 1973, has turned out to be (on the whole) a flexible and efficacious instrument for accommodating the new capital exporters and the major semi-industrialized capital importers. But present arrangements remain historically anomalous and vulnerable in several ways. Besides the contrasts already noted between new and old capital exporters, consider the following points:

a) The level of OPEC capital exports depends heavily on the real price of oil, rather than on stable long-term saving and investment propensities. During 1974 through 1977 OPEC surpluses were large, but tending to decrease until 1978, when they practically disappeared; in 1979 they rose sharply once again. For many importers of both oil and capital it is unclear whether the inflows are adding to productive capacity or simply maintaining consumption above levels sustainable in the long run (assuming the persistence of high real energy prices). Contrary to much historical experience in the periphery, worsening terms of trade accompany the capital inflow.

b) The 1973—80 "recycling" was aided by "money mirage" on the part of capital exporters. *Ex-post* real yields on dollar-denominated financial assets were low, certainly lower than the yield on oil in the ground. One wonders how long such a money mirage can last. Yet insistence by capital exporters on positive real rates of return on their financial assets would add to the problems of capital importers.

c) Political relations between old and new capital exporters are far from harmonious. Tensions between Iran and the USA, leading to the freeze in 1979 of Iranian assets in US-owned banks, had important negative repercussions in the syndicated Euro-currency market. Catastrophic scenarios are much too easily imagined.

Systemic Issues for the 1980s

The expansion of international capital markets, the adoption of floating exchange rates, and the macroeconomic difficulties of many industrialized countries have encouraged the re-examination of academic and practical orthodoxies, as well as some Southern heterodoxies. Already during the late 1950s Northern academic centers witnessed a rebirth of interest in monetary and financial topics. Northern macroeconomic and monetary theories encountered sharp debates during the 1960s, leading to a surge of neomonetarist and neoclassical positions in the 1970s. It would be difficult to talk about a monolithic Northern academic (or even practical) orthodoxy on such issues as the desirability of flexible exchange rates, optimum controls over capital movements, the correct strategy to combat inflation, or the necessity of regulation over the Eurocurrency market. In these matters there is a "great disorder under heaven". Under these circumstances one may hear Raul Prebisch castigate the evils of international inflation with greater vigor than James Tobin, and find that Robert Mundell defends fixed exchange rates with greater ardor than Antonio Delfim Netto. At a more practical level it is not unusual to find Southern exporters together with Northern bankers (worried about debt service) singing the praises of freer world trade, while Northern trade unionists, together with their "progressive" academic advisers, rediscover all sorts of heterodox arguments for protection.

The Eurocurrency market and international bank lending during the 1970s displayed a number of features which compare favorably with earlier capital market arrangements from the viewpoint of at least some important semi-industrialized countries (as well as several socialist countries). Probably no international capital market in history has had a lower degree of political interference, to the dismay of "strategic minds" like that of Dr. Henry Kissinger. Competition among banks has been keen and, as already noted, *ex-post* interest rates and charges do not seem unreasonable. In contrast with pre-1929 Brazilian experience in the New York market, members of the Bogota group, which combined major coffee producers, have borrowed freely to finance their price stabilization operations. Officials in several semi-industrialized countries have been able to ignore IMF advice without seeing their external credit lines dry up.

It is also clear that the 1973—80 international capital market has contributed little to transferring resources to the poorest countries in the Periphery. It can also be argued that the market still has a number of important gaps limiting its usefulness even to semi-industrialized countries.[7] Persistent and erratic inflation in the country of the central currency in international payments, the US dollar, tends to increase uncertainty and reduce maturities, and raises the need for a greater role for financial instruments denominated in other strong currencies.

Although quite competitive, the Eurocurrency market, and more generally international bank lending, are alleged to have a number of structural imperfections calling for official regulation. For some years it was argued that the Eurocurrency market generated explosive increases in world credit, significantly adding to world inflation. This view is now mostly discredited; Alexander Swoboda recently concluded that: "If the concern is to moderate inflation in the world economy, focus on the regulation of the Eurodollar market carries with it the danger that the forest will be missed for the trees."[8] The case for greater control, or at least supervision, over all international bank lending essentially rests on the argument that if Northern governments (explicitly or implicitly) insure depositors against all of the consequences of possible bank failures, and politically important borrowers against default, then "moral hazard" imperfections may exist, i.e., banks may be less careful in their choice of loans than without government "insurance". It is also noted that, at present, supervision over Eurocurrency lending is less than over the rest of international lending, a difference difficult to justify on *a priori* grounds.

The financial press and speeches of bankers are also full of references to deteriorating capital-asset ratios of banks engaged in international lending. Typically, it is concluded that higher profit margins are needed for reinvestment so as to bolster the capital-asset ratios. These remarks take for granted (a) that entry of *new* banks into international lending is either slow or non-existent; and (b) that capital cannot grow by other means than the reinvestment of profit. Moreover, the microeconomic rationale for rules-of-thumb about capital-asset ratios is obscure at best; in practice, US and non-US banks have very different ratios.

The international loan market, in contrast with, say, international non-oil commodity markets, is an area where nowadays market imperfections are perceived more clearly in the North than in the South. At first sight it is remarkable how bankers plead for more official lending to LDCs, i.e., seek actions that can take business away from them, and argue in favor of greater bureaucratic control over markets, i.e., seek a larger IMF role in the lending process. (One may contrast this puzzle with that generated by OPEC exhorting its customers to conserve oil.) What is sought, of course, is a "rationalization" of lending under IMF planning to reduce "cut-throat" competition. This has already been achieved for state-subsidized export credits, with OECD countries agreeing (with periodic "lapses" into competition) to guidelines on interest floors, maximum credit periods, and minimum cash payments.

Increased international banking competition, under conditions of expanding oil-related credit supplies and a large accumulated debt of non-oil LDCs, creates an important latent demand for technical arguments favoring a Northern-directed rationalization of international capital markets. Supply will not take long to respond, with the practical orthodoxy unearthing all sorts of externalities, distortions and market imperfections to justify Northern regulation over private financial flows to non-oil LDCs and to socialist countries.

In this context, semi-industrialized LDCs which are heavy borrowers from banks face dilemmas of both an economic and a political nature.

From an economic standpoint, the unregulated credit markets of 1973—80 presented great advantages, but such markets may not persist in the 1980s. Oligopolistic forces of restraint may prevail over competitive tendencies to expand in private international banking. As a result, the large volume of credit required by semi-industrialized LDCs, particularly in the early 1980s, may not be forthcoming as expected from the private banking system. GNP growth rates may suffer as a consequence. Behavioral characteristics of private international financial intermediaries may thus have a critical influence on feasible growth rates for semi-industrialized LDCs; this is illustrated in the Appendix.

From a political perspective, semi-industrialized non-oil LDCs have alternative options depending on expected international scenarios. Under conditions of relative tranquility, they may bet that, without the acquiescence of themselves and of OPEC lenders, industrial country governments and private bankers will not be able to find a *modus operandi* for effective regulation of international banking activities. In this case, those countries may choose to play a maverick role, maximizing their borrowing opportunities, and leaving those who dominate the system to worry about systemic issues.

However, OPEC (especially its members with the largest surpluses) may be induced to form a coalition with industrial countries and private banks, to regulate world capital markets, perhaps under the IMF umbrella, according to their own immediate interest. Any incipient financial crisis is likely to accelerate the formation of such a coalition. OPEC would obtain "sound and remunerative financial assets" and private banks would enjoy "orderly market conditions" in which higher interest costs and spreads could be passed on to borrowers with nowhere else to go. Industrial countries would obtain steadier oil flows as OPEC trades oil underground for the safe financial asset. At marginal costs, approval of the Fourth World could be obtained to give an appearance of legitimacy to this re-establishment of Northern control over international financial flows. Note that part of the motivation for the proposed Substitution Account at the IMF was to meet OPEC's dissatisfaction with available financial assets.[9] This financial arrangement would be the counterpart of the coalition between OPEC and the traditional oil multinationals, which operates with great tensions and frictions but has been enormously profitable for both sides so far.

Semi-industrialized countries may want to anticipate the new financial coalition, combining their own forces to seek to bargain for rules for the international financial game which for them will be inferior to the present free-for-all system, but better than the arrangements that would be set up by creditors under conditions of financial strain. At present, it is not clear which of these alternative strategies these countries should opt for.

Latin American financial policies and problems

The analyses of the previous sections suggest that on balance semi-industrialized countries were not hurt by the emergence and expansion of private international financial markets. True enough, the costs of private credits were higher and of a shorter-term nature than official bilateral or multilateral finance. However, volumes were larger, procedures were more expeditious, and strings attached — both at the political and at the economic policy levels — were looser.

Financial intermediation rose to pre-eminence in Latin America (LA) along with blossoming international capital markets. A practical orthodoxy developed, preaching that "the more financial intermediation the better". Gurley and Shaw popularized correlation measures between the degree of financial modernization and indexes of economic development. Ronald McKinnon argued vigorously against "financial repression". New technocrats rose in the 1970s to policy-making positions in Southern Cone governments and started implementing policies of financial liberalization. Brazil, Colombia and Mexico followed more pragmatic policy courses but, in all these countries, foreign finance influenced the rhythm of economic activity and the nature of government policy-making during the 1970s.

143

Relevant questions of a socio-economic nature, which we now briefly review, have been raised concerning these new forms of LA financial interaction with the capitalist world economy.

De-regulation of financial markets led to the loss by old-style banking of market-power to adventuresome but capital-short "financieras". Under these conditions, lack of government insurance of depositors frequently resulted in a string of financial panics and scandals, the regulatory sequel of which tended to strengthen the oligopolistic character of the banking sector.

These movements were accompanied by a substantial increase in the share of financial intermediation in the national economies. There seems to have been a tendency towards the centralization of capital in the hands of economic groups with a banking basis. "Old" industrialists lost economic power to "new" financiers. Some LA economists feared that the banking sector would go through a process of de-nationalization, as multinational banks benefited from de-regulation to enter a market where previously only domestic residents were allowed. However, domestic economic groups proved to be more active than anticipated by these economists; financial liberalization apparently proceeded along with new forms of association between domestic and foreign capital, rather than with a massive take-over of the former by the latter.

Other economists were concerned with the possibility that this substitution of "financial capital" for "productive capital" would impart a stagnationist bias to the financial liberalization policies implemented in the Southern Cone. We argue below that some Keynesian problems do emerge in this context, but they are probably of a short to medium term nature not of a long-run stagnationist variety. Nonetheless, it is hard to see what good the feverish speculative activity of the very short-term financial markets that were allowed to develop in countries like Argentina can do for production. In this context, one should remember Kenneth J. Arrow's point: "... in speculative markets such as those for stocks and commodity futures, a large amount invested in the acquisition of new information for private advantage will yield no social gain, only a zero-sum redistribution ... We may have very able people who could be useful spending their time in production instead of trying to outwit others".[10]

The progressive loss of government control over monetary aggregates in a context of openness to international financial markets confused policy-makers and economic analysts alike. Old style monetarists had to recycle themselves to get rid of their preoccupation with active monetary policy, reluctantly accepting the idea of an endogenous money supply. Structuralist economists, on the other hand, had to wrestle with their old propositions regarding passive money to become active partisans of sterilization policies in the context of a financially open economy.

In the Southern Cone, the "middle-age Chicago" eventually prevailed over the "old Chicago", and policy-makers there, while furthering the processes of trade and financial liberalization, started aiming at fixed nominal exchange rates associated with zero budget deficits. Pragmatism continued to characterize Brazilian and Colombian policy-making. With varying degrees of success, these countries attempted to stick with the "crawling peg" without explicit targets and to maintain seigniorage over the monetary base, by restricting access of domestic residents to international financial markets. Mexico wanted to follow a similar path, but in her case the task of avoiding currency substitution was made much more difficult than in Brazil or Colombia in view of her geographical and economic proximity to the USA.

The existence of a fluid international financial market, by changing the nature of economic incentives and penalties, forced LA economies into a new mold during the 1970s. In principle, it extended the range of options opened to economic policy-making, hence providing new opportunities for economic gain. But it also twisted the system of economic incentives in particular directions (and we have already mentioned some shifts of relative economic power that it brought about). In this context, the rules of access established by domestic policy-makers seem to have been a basic determinant of the short to medium term consequences of financial openness. The returns are not all in yet, but from our present perspective, it seems that countries that followed a more pragmatic and gradualistic course of action (such as Brazil and Colombia) have done better than countries that pursued a more doctrinaire and abrupt policy course (as in the Southern Cone).

The use of indexed government bonds is a characteristic feature of the financial reforms that have accompanied the process of financial opening in the LA context. In the remainder of this section, we discuss some Keynesian conundrums evoked by the experience of countries following this policy path.

According to the financial reformers, increased availability of financial paper paying positive real interest rates should both increase the flow of private saving and divert wealth holding away from nonproductive uses (land, housing, consumer durables) and into productive assets.

Latin American experiences with financial reform confirm the prediction on the increase of financial saving; however, private productive investment did not react accordingly. The marginal propensity to save goes up, but private investment rates are not larger than before. This reaction to financial reform has been accompanied by persistently high inflation rates, lagging exchange rates, and increasing foreign debts. Reasons for these Latin American aberrations are not entirely clear, but some of their aspects are worth exploring.

We consider, successively, stylized versions of the portfolio decisions relating to the composition of domestic-currency-denominated assets, and of the portfolio decisions concerning the distribution of wealth between domestic and international assets — before and after "financial liberation".

In a financially repressed economy with a history of persistent inflation, wealth is held as money, land and capital. In relative terms, the first two are homogeneous commodities, whereas the latter is a collection of heterogeneous goods. Money is held because of its property as a means of payment; capital, because of its expected yield in use; and land, as a shelter against inflation. Expected land yields may be low, but they are strongly correlated with inflation rates; thus land is safer to hold than heterogeneous capital. The liquidity of land is higher than that of capital but much lower than that of money. The yield of the latter is strongly negative. Lack of a high yielding asset with a strong secondary market presumably underlies low observed saving propensities. Moreover, a high proportion of net additions to wealth take the form of unproductive land holdings for "speculative" purposes.

In this context, financial reform-mongers typically propose introducing an indexed government bond as an instrument of financial liberation. (In McKinnon's terminology this boils down to paying real interest rates on "money".) In the presence of such an attractive asset with a strong back-up market, saving propensities should increase and a higher proportion of wealth should be held as "productive" capital. An implicit hypothesis seems to be that the bond will protect wealth-owners against inflation better than land holdings do. Hence, the required real rate of return on capital will be lower and thus capital accumulation will be favored for a given state of long-term expectations.

As has been seen, Latin American experience supports the presumption on saving propensities but not the expectation on private investment rates. The apparent reason is that indexed bonds tend to replace capital (and money) rather than land in private portfolio holdings. Free-market-oriented financial reforms are accompanied by a general liberalization of interest rates, in the context of a demand-contractionary package of policies. Bankruptcies in the productive sector and panics and scandals in the financial sector are frequent. As a consequence, there is a weakening in the state of confidence with which expectations about future capital values are held. Long-term expectations collapse, the demand price of capital falls, and the rate of investment adjusts downwards at a time when saving propensities are on the increase. High short-term interest rates tend to raise the supply price of output in the short run. An excess supply of money may also obtain, in spite of contractionary monetary policies, if the demand for money (in the appropriate M_1 concept) is sufficiently lowered by the introduction of indexed bonds. Continuing high inflation rates, higher unemployment rates, and lower growth rates of potential output are the short to medium term consequences of ill-implemented financial reforms.

Similar problems may occur with respect to the portfolio decisions regarding dollar- *vis-à-vis* peso-denominated wealth. Capital market reformers correctly expect that the creation of domestic indexed bonds will induce (foreign as well as national) wealth-owners to shift a higher proportion of their wealth out of dollar- and into peso-denominated assets. Experience confirms that *ex-ante* foreign savings are larger than before, as predicted by the theory, but also that they do not find a real outlet, since domestic absorption goes down following the mechanism sketched in the previous paragraph. Capital account surpluses are not compensated for by correspondingly larger full-capacity current account deficits. Official foreign reserves accumulate and exchange rates lag behind purchasing power parities. The "retraso cambiario" established itself, weakening the propensity to export and strengthening the propensity to import: paradoxically enough, the level of activity in the tradable goods sector shrinks in order to absorb the increased flow of foreign savings.

Portfolio reshuffling favoring government debt is a common characteristic of these examples of financial reform. If the government uses the proceeds of higher bond sales either to increase its own investment or to subsidize private investment, real income growth may be maintained, at the cost of increased government intervention in the economic sphere and expanding foreign debt. If the proceeds of higher bond sales are used to control the growth rate of money supply, inflation rates may subside but the rate of investment and potential output growth do not recover.

Academic orthodoxy, from Maynard Keynes to James Tobin, has taught that the propensity to invest is not coterminous with the propensity to save. Lack of attention to this basic teaching on the part of practical orthodoxy may explain the failures of recent attempts at financial reform in Latin America. Much research is needed on the patterns of substitution and complementarity among assets, in the context of high and varying rates of inflation characteristic of Latin American countries.

Appendix

GNPs, Current Accounts and Financial Intermediation

The interactions of GNP (or GNP growth), current account positions, and the preferences of international financial intermediaries are illustrated on page 150. Assume the world is divided into three regions: OPEC, OECD, and non-OPEC LDCs. Assume further that OPEC GNP (or its growth) is exogenously given by the development plans of those countries, and that the real oil price is also given. The OPEC current account surplus (OA) will then depend on non-OPEC GNP (or its growth, from now on denoted as Y), and its composition between LDC Y and OECD Y.

The negatively sloping line YY^1 gives the OPEC surplus corresponding to a given non-OPEC Y; if oil requirements per unit of Y were equal in LDCs and OECD, the line would be vertical. For each non-OPEC Y there will be a different line YY. The vertical axis gives LDC Y relative to OECD Y; at this ratio increases (maintaining constant their weighted sum to yield a given non-OPEC Y), it is assumed that the OPEC surplus will decline, i.e., that there is a greater use of oil per unit of Y in OECD than in LDCs.

The positively sloping lines in the diagram show the level and structure of the LDC current account deficit. The difference between the two lines represents the LDC deficit with OPEC. The LDC deficit with OECD is assumed to depend solely on the ratio of LDC Y to OECD Y. The LDC deficit with OPEC will increase as LDC Y increases, so the total LDC deficit will increase as LDC Y increases with a given non-OPEC Y. The diagram supposes that, during the time-span relevant for our analysis, adjustment mechanisms other

148

than changes in Y can do little to affect the structure of world current account deficits and surpluses.

Consider first a borderline situation when the OPEC surplus OA is exactly matched by an LDC overall deficit of equal amount, made up of an LDC deficit with OECD of OB and an LDC deficit with OPEC of BA. OECD then has a deficit with OPEC of OB. Supposing that all capital movements are handled by international financial intermediaries (i.e., assume away grants, direct investments, etc.), those institutions will witness an increase in their net claims on non-OPEC LDCs equal to OA, matched by increased OPEC claims on the intermediaries.

Consider now a situation when after several years of accumulating claims on LDCs, the financial intermediaries decide that it would be "imprudent" to maintain the same rate of accumulation. A possible outcome, for a given non-OPEC Y, would be a reduction in LDC Y and an increase in OECD Y, from OZ to OW. In the new situation financial intermediaries would reduce their accumulation on LDC debts to OB, while accumulating more reliable OECD paper at a rate of BD. The OECD will become a capital importer. A more likely possibility avoiding an increse in the OPEC surplus would involve both a reduction of non-OPEC Y (leading to a shift of YY to the left) and a reduction of LDC Y relative to OECD Y.

For a given non-OPEC Y, an increase in the real price of oil would be depicted in Figure 1 by a shift to the right of YY[1]. An opposite shift would result from an increase in the development plans of OPEC. Neither an increase in oil prices nor in OPEC Y would shift the line showing the LDC deficit with OECD, but would of course shift (to the right for oil price increases, to the left for OPEC Y increase) the line showing the overall LDC deficit, reflecting changes in the balance of payments between LDCs and OPEC. The shifts in the line depicting the overall LDC deficit would be horizontally smaller than the YY[1] shifts.

More vigorous conservation policies would shift YY[1] to the left; its slope will change if those efforts are proportionally different in LDCs and OECD. LDC conservation efforts would also be reflected in a leftward shift in the line indicating its total current account deficit.

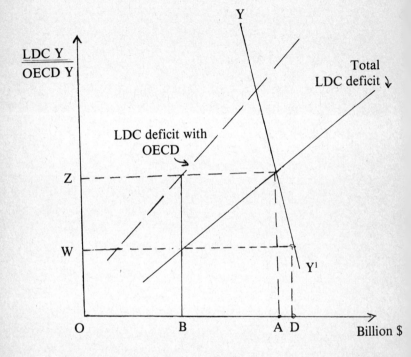

Figure 1

Notes

1 See especially Celso Furtado, *Formacao Economica da America Latina,* Lia Editor S.A, Rio de Janeiro, 1969, Chapter IX.

2 For a fascinating analysis of the Montagu Mission see Winston Fritsch, 1924, in ANPEC, *VII Encontro Nacional de Economia,* Vol. 2, Atibaia, Sao Paulo, 11—14 December 1979, pp. 673—732.

3 See Charles P. Kindleberger, "The cyclical pattern of long-term lending", mimeographed, M.I.T., 1980, pp. 6—9.

4 Marcelo de Paiva Abreu, "O Brasil e a economia mundial, 1929—1945", mimeographed, Rio de Janeiro, 1980.

5 Marcelo de Paiva Abreau, "A Missao Niemeyer", *Revisita de Administracao de Empresas,* Rio de Janeiro, July/August 1974, p. 15. The United Kingdom abandoned the gold standard in September 1931.

6 See M.S. Mendelsohn, *Money on the Move: The Modern International Capital Market,* New York: McGraw-Hill Books Company, 1980, p. 55.

7 See the report of the Independent Commission on International Development Issued under the Chairmanship of Willy Brandt, *North-South: A Programme for Survival,* London, Pan Books, 1980, Chapters 14 and 15.

8 Alexander K. Swoboda, *Credit Creation in the Euromarket: Alternative Theories and Implications for Control,* Group of Thirty, Occasional Papers, 2, New York, 1980.

9 See the address by J. de Larosiere, Managing Director of the IMF, in the *IMF Survey* for 3 June, 1980, especially pp. 173—4.

10 Quoted from *Challenge,* Sept/Oct 1979, pp. 26—7.

Part IV

Economic Theory and the General Practice of International Economic Policy

Chapter 9

OECD Theory in North-South Practice

Richard Jolly

The core of OECD's economic theory may be defined as "coordinated demand management along the grain of the free-market and open international trading system": in essence, Keynes plus neoclassical resource allocation theory. Practice is often, of course, something different — the result not only of the pressures and specific policies of member states, but of eclectic and of what I would term structural approaches in particular studies or departments of the OECD. Nevertheless, the core of Keynesian macro and neoclassical micro theory for long guided the public philosophy and policy proposals of the Secretariat in the annual Ministerial Meetings of the OECD, the periodic ECSS (Executive Committee in Special Session) meetings, and in most of the other work undertaken by the Directorate of Economic Affairs. More recently, it seems that the Keynesian element of demand management has been sacrificed in the anti-inflationary battle, guided by quasi-monetarist philosophies.

The bulk of OECD's analytical work has been short-term rather than medium-term, let alone long-term. It was only in 1978 that OECD first undertook formal econometric projections extending more than 18 or 24 months ahead. This is — or ought to be — surprising, in that the very origins of the OECD, or strictly those of the OEEC, which preceded it, are derived from the Marshall Plan in 1948, which expressly required participating European countries to set up planning and coordinating units, which in turn gave rise to a series of five-year national plans and planning structures, some of which are still operating, as in Norway and Sweden.

As regards North-South relations, OECD has acted as a coordinating forum for a number of years for the Group B countries, notably at and following the CIEC, Avenue Kleber negotiations in 1976—77. Formal coordination was placed in the ECSS and, at least in 1978, more than half of the time spent in ECSS meetings was given to North-South issues — a remarkable fact, given that the ECSS is the most senior economic committee of the OECD, with responsibilities also for broad coordination of economic policy among the OECD member states themselves.

By 1978 a consensus had emerged within the ECSS that OECD's response to the North-South dialogue had too often been reactive rather than constructive — and that the elements of a more positive approach should be worked out and put forward, based on the OECD's own interests. Accordingly, an attempt was made to clarify the issues and to define the basis for such a positive approach.

As a short-stay participant in the process — formally employed as a special consultant to the Secretary-General, I can only give a partial, personal, and no doubt highly inadequate view of the process of turning theory into practice. Nevertheless, the three main initiatives taken that year — the preparation of a general paper defining the basis of a constructive approach to North-South relationships, a study of the NICs (the newly industrialized countries) and on positive adjustment, and a proposal for stepped-up investment, are worth reviewing, because of the light they shed on some major concerns in North-South relations and on the way OECD theory helps or hinders analysis and policy formulation to deal with them. The experience is also of continuing interest because those three topics bear close relationship to some of the central proposals put forward in the Brandt report, though admittedly presented in that document in a more coherent and comprehensive manner. An analysis of the OECD experience in 1978 may therefore be a useful case study.

Background and developments

A specific call for a new approach to North-South relationships on the part of the OECD was put forward in 1976 by President Kreisky, who called for a major increase in transfers from the OECD to the developing countries as a stimulus both to development and to the OECD economies themselves at a time of considerable under-utilization of resources. In October 1977 at the annual high level meeting of the DAC (Development Assistance Committee), Secretary of State Stoltenberg of Norway and Judith Hart, Minister of Overseas Development in Britain, reiterated the proposal and asked that the OECD Secretariat undertake fundamental work to explore the idea.

In fact, little serious work was undertaken, largely because the proposal was seen as a "non-starter" — an irrelevant distraction which on occasion was even termed "a stupid idea". The proposal was usually rejected on first principles: that the Keynesian stimulus implied by the proposal would be too small and too long delayed to be worth serious consideration by the OECD countries; and that politically it was a non-starter, since if the OECD Secretariat was unable to get German and Japanese support for an *intra*-OECD Keynesian stimulus, of either a "locomotive" or later a "convoy" variety, there seemed to be no chance that it could get support for similar measures whose first-round beneficiaries would be *outside* the OECD.

At the April meeting of the ECSS in 1978 a position paper was put forward outlining a positive and constructive approach to the developing countries by the OECD members, based on three guiding principles:

"(a) the requirements for the efficient management of inter-dependence within the world economy;

  (b) a medium/long-term view of the sorts of changes in structure and balance within the world economy which both the industrial countries and the developing countries would consider desirable;

  (c) a commitment to a continuing and evolving approach to development cooperation, which would clearly go beyond the strict needs of economic interdependence to strengthen the capacity of developing countries to participate less inequitably within the world economy and to provide for accelerated development in the poorer parts of the world, if possible within some broad frame of objectives for the next decade or two."

Several points were emphasized in elaboration of this approach. First, it was to be applied in a dynamic and forward-looking framework — not as the maintenance of the *status quo* but as the management of interdependence in an evolving and developing context. Second, it suggested the need to build on areas where there existed positive gains for both the industrialized and the developing countries, if the issues were to be effectively dealt with. Third, it recognized the need for institutional changes and policies to protect countries against excessive vulnerability to the vicissitudes of the international economic environment. Fourth, it put the emphasis on objectives to be jointly achieved and not only on means and processes, especially with respect to areas of medium- or longer-run structural change in the global economy, where North and South shared mutual interests.

The paper was preliminary, but illustrated its proposed approach by reference to energy, where, it was argued, the OECD member countries, the OPEC nations, and the non-OPEC oil-importing developing countries shared a number of common interests in moving towards less reliance on non-renewable energy supplies and towards conservation and development of further sources of energy. A brief mention was also made of transfers as a way of stimulating structural changes in this and other sectors — but still the paper lacked a central point of focus. In preliminary discussion of the paper within the ECSS it was suggested that further work needed to be done to give specific content to its proposals.

A major step forward took place in the informal "Tidewater" meeting in early April, at which ministers of development of a number of DAC countries met with McNamara, Brandt and two Third Worlders, Ramphal the Secretary-General of the Commonwealth, and Al-Hamad, the Director-General of the OPEC Special Fund. The Kreisky and Hart proposals were again discussed, this time informally and with strong support from a number of those present. Although doubts were voiced, the Secretary-General of OECD returned convinced that the ideas deserved serious consideration. A major shift then occurred within the Secretariat, or at least amongst the limited number of persons mainly concerned. A flurry of drafts were prepared over the next few weeks for a proposal for stepped-up investment, which would involve a major programme of transfers, building up to net additional flows of about $10 billion within three or four years, mobilizing both OPEC surpluses and under-utilized private savings within the OECD countries, directed towards sectors (especially energy, commodities and agriculture) where the OECD countries shared a mutual interest in structural change. The institutional mechanisms for stimulating the financial flow were far from fully defined at this point, though within a few weeks, reliance on co-financing between the international financial institutions and private banks under the umbrella of the World Bank and the Regional Development Banks in particular became central.

A first draft of the proposal was discussed at a special meeting of DAC in late May, a speedy scheduling made possible by strong leadership by the Chairman, Maurice Williams, who had also prepared the agenda for the Tidewater meeting a few weeks earlier. Unfortunately, the tight time-table meant that few countries had sufficient time to consider their positions. In the event — and as so often in international discussions before and since — discussion was supportive of further work in this area, but cautious and inconclusive

158

about immediate action. Several countries were also cautious about the idea of focussing on specific sectors — as opposed to using the additional transfers for the support of any useful development project.

Within the Secretariat and in particular with the support of the Secretary-General, the proposal had by then emerged as a centre piece for the Ministerial meetings scheduled for mid-June — an annual date in the OECD calendar at which there is always a premium on putting forward some fresh proposals, new enough to stimulate a sense of progress, but not so specific or radical as to cause serious threat of action. In preparation for this, discussions of the proposal for stepped-up investment were held by the Chairman of DAC and other Secretariat members involved, with leading members of the banking community in the USA, West Germany, and Britain. Inevitably there were mixed views on specifics, but strong support was declared in general for the main lines of the proposal among OECD member countries, although clear differences among different countries were emerging. The Dutch and the Scandinavians were strongly encouraging, pressing for further work as well as, in the case of Sweden, undertaking independent study within their own Foreign Ministry for direct submission to the Committee of the Whole meeting in New York.

In the event, the Ministerial discussion in mid-June was again supportive of further study, but again cautious over early action. The more specific elements of the proposal, particularly those relating to its size, its sectors of concentration, and the need for Southern as well as Northern participation in any mechanism to oversee it, were removed or whittled down to an ambiguous phrase. The Ministerial communiqué issued to the members for the meeting, like the communiqué issued after the 1978 Summit of Heads of State in Bonn a month later, made explicit reference to the proposal, but in the form of half a sentence, which only those who knew the inside story would really recognize.

Over the next nine months, the proposal was further refined, studied, debated, laundered and redrafted, to the point where, in Spring 1979, a modest paper emerged and was eventually made public. This outlined the issues and suggested that a measure of additional cofinancing between the World Bank and the private sector might play a useful role in the years ahead. But no figures were given and most of the other specific elements were removed or so qualified as to have little effect. In any case, by then the World Bank had approved internally a programme for a modest increase in co-financing from a level of $0.5 billion to perhaps $1.5—2 billion.

In a less official way, though more publicly, parallel and more comprehensive proposals were by then being prepared by the Brandt Commission. Brandt's Emergency programme for 1980—5 released in March 1980, contained four elements:

1. A large-scale transfer of resources to developing countries;
2. An international energy strategy;
3. A global food programme;
4. A start on some major reforms in the international economic system.

The first three of these elements, and some of Brandt's other proposals, closely parallel those of these OECD documents — though generally Brandt has been bolder, more comprehensive, and less qualified. In particular, Brandt's large-scale transfers were to build up to an additional $50—60 billion by 1985, and to be half concessional and half non-concessional. The restraining influences of theory on the more modest sort of OECD proposals are all the more interesting — precisely because, in the different context of an international commission, bolder and more comprehensive proposals were more readily accepted.

A major preoccupation of the OECD countries over this period concerning international economic issues was competition between the major economies of the OECD. This was recognized within the OECD Secretariat, at least with respect to the exporting strength of West Germany and Japan. Indeed, a major reason for undertaking the study of the NICs was to set out the facts of Japan's growing export performance — which, in its impact on the world export shares of the rest of the already-industrialized countries of the OECD, equalled the combined share of the 11 main NICs taken together.

Free and unfettered competition was, in principle, the accepted principle of the free market system of the OECD — and thus interventions to set limits on the competitive power of West Germany and Japan were unthinkable to OECD, or so it was formally said. Yet practice, as so often, was clearly different from principle — from "theory" or ideology. Most OECD countries at the time, and for several if not many years previously, were involved in a whole series of tariff and non-tariff barriers in restraint of international trade. Even while solemnly renewing their annual pledge in favour of free trade, countries would recognize that its implementation was made more difficult by growing unemployment and were informally engaged in market-sharing discussions. Given this, the critical question is why the OECD countries were not able to recognize openly these trade-offs and to devise collective action *both* to achieve higher levels of employment in the shorter run *and* to maintain international competition and resource allocation according to principles of comparative advantage in the longer run.

Some would argue that this was not possible, because such measures would be against the interests of those in the strongest positions — either nations, notably West Germany or Japan, or corporations. Such explanations, to my mind, show too little appreciation of the orders of magnitude of what was being lost in growth, since capacity utilization and employment were all at levels significantly below what might have been achieved. The losses were not small, but huge, $200 billion a year for the OECD countries as a whole was an informal estimate within the Secretariat. Probably this is a considerable underestimate (e.g., to judge by Okun's Law) — yet even by this estimate, the cumulative losses over the succession of years in which high unemployment was tolerated are staggering.

The role of theory in the practice

There are at least three basic questions to ask when trying to interpret the role of theory in this experience — the birth, life and institutional death of an initiative in practice.

1. To what extent did dominant OECD theory divert attention from critical problems or inhibit effective action?
2. To what extent was existing theory adequate to the task of better understanding what seemed to be the factors involved, whether economic or political?
3. To what extent was theory simply irrelevant to the issues that in practice encouraged or obstructed action?

All three questions raise the old issue as to whether theory ever provides an independent frame of analysis or merely one that reflects or rationalizes the underlying interests of the parties involved. Joan Robinson in *Economic Philosophy* (1962) saw the leading economic theories of the last two hundred years as reflecting little more than the interest of the dominant economic classes of the time. Marx saw theory as part of the "superstructure", a rationalization that simply reflected the underlying class interests. Regardless of whether one accepts or rejects these general positions, it is difficult not to recognize that OECD's espousal of Keynes plus the free and open trading system broadly matches the interests of the dominant OECD countries. But at the same time, it is also difficult not to see areas and periods where feedback from theory to policy to action had impeded quite powerful interests, at least within the short and medium run. And, as I shall emphasize, which interests and whose interests are important questions, the answers to which are far from obvious.

(a) Where did theory inhibit action?

In the events described, this seemed to arise in two major cases. First, with respect to structural change, there had within OECD been a long-fought battle — or perhaps, guerilla skirmishes with an entrenched power — as to whether or not the concept of structural problems and imbalances had any meaning, let alone any relevance, for the OECD economies. The dominant position, put forward by the Directorate of Economic Affairs, was that structural imbalance had no identifiable meaning. There were no basic rigidities or imbalances which changes in price would not ultimately resolve. The economies were flexible and, providing the market was allowed to operate, self-adjusting mechanisms would come into play. As late as January 1978, it was possible for a leading OECD economist to state that the basic problem was to restore growth. If the OECD countries could get back to 5 percent growth, he argued, most of the problems currently called structural would disappear. Even if some structural problems remained, they would be slight and certainly energy would not be one of them.

This position was strongly under attack from two quarters within OECD. Many of the country representatives argued that structural imbalances were serious problems for their own countries which the Directorate should work on. In addition, within a number of Directorates concerned with particular sectors, and as a minority group within the Economic Affairs Directorate, there were professionals, including professional economists, arguing the importance of structural imbalances.

These elements of support made it possible for the general outline of a new approach to North-South relations, and for the programme of stepped-up investment in particular, to focus on structural change between North and South as a desirable goal of the proposals, in the interests of the North as well as the South. (It must of course be recognized that acceptance of stepped-up investment in agriculture, energy and commodities would also have been feasible on straight grounds of increasing Third World production, whether or not international structural imbalances in these sectors were independently seen to be genuine issues of concern.) Nevertheless, by mid-1979, the need for the OECD Directorate to undertake a more explicit programme of analyses of structural problems within the OECD economies had been accepted as part of the work programme for the following year.

Acceptance of some work on structural problems should not be seen as a major concession to structural analysis. The work on "positive adjustment policies" remained closely within a neoclassical frame of analysis, and its main conclusions for policy were negative ones — to stop intervening in the market rather than to intervene more constructively guided by long-run objectives. Although such issues were explored in OECD's major Interfutures project, this project remained peripheral to the mainstream economic work of OECD, and its emphasis on long-run structural issues rather than comparative advantage was an explicit point for which it was criticized by mainstream OECD economists.

The second area where theory proved inhibiting was in the concept of inequitable relationships between developed and developing countries, and the need for special measures, and for OECD support, to offset them. The April 1978 draft of the basic paper proposing a new approach to North-South relations came in for specific criticism on this point, with questions raised about the ambiguity and meaningfulness of seeking to make relationships between countries less inequitable. ("In what sense", it was once put to me, "is an economic relationship between Chad and the United States any less equal than one between Germany and the United States?") After long discussion, among government representatives and separately within the Secretariat, it was agreed that the original proposal should be amended to read "to enable the developing countries to participate more fully" rather than "less unequally", let alone less inequitably, within the world economy. In one specific area, however, that of restrictive business practices, there was strong and widespread agreement that economic relationships might be inadequate and that the OECD ought to recognize the need for action to deal with them.

Apart from these two specific areas, OECD's general theoretical stance, by expecting market responses to be self-adjusting, generally acts to inhibit specific policy interventions. In the context of North-

South relationships, this creates a presumption against intervention, except to make markets work more efficiently, and for "aid", on the grounds that aid is conceptually the international equivalent of a domestic transfer payment, justified theoretically as a necessary mechanism to achieve a more satisfactory distributional outcome than market resource allocation alone can achieve.

(b) Where more relevant theory was needed

So far we have looked at areas where theory inhibited analysis or action. The second and related question is: where were there problems that more relevant theory might have helped to analyse? This, of course, is sometimes the opposite side of the previous coin: where existing theory inhibits analysis or action, more relevant theory might assist.

In the cases in question, there were four critical aspects that desperately needed convincing, definitive analysis, which, in the event, never emerged.

First, the inflationary impact of the proposed programme of stepped-up investment or massive transfers. Looked at through monetarist eyes, inflation might be stimulated in a number of ways. Looked at through Keynesian eyes, inflationary tendencies would arise primarily through supply bottlenecks in sectors where demand might rise more than the extent of existing undercapacity utilization or through a general decline of unemployment producing an upward tendency on prices, through some Phillips-curve mechanism. Both approaches might lead to offsetting tendencies, especially in the medium run, through higher levels of activity and lower levels of unemployment, easing rigidities in the labour or factor or product markets. But although much was presumed about these issues, both the analytical work needed to clarify the application of the theories to the situations in question and empirical material needed to assess their relevance or quantitative impact were almost totally lacking. It was largely, as so often on fundamental issues, theological argument from first principles, rather than empirical science.

A second and closely related issue was "absorptive capacity" within the developing countries and excess capacity within the industrial countries. In spite of a number of international studies which estimated total investment needs in agriculture, energy and mineral development in developing countries as $25 billion or more a year, doubts were continually raised about the ability of these countries to absorb additional investment building up to a level of $10 billion within three or four years. In parallel, doubts were raised about the capacity of export industries in the North to supply additional goods, without reaching the limits of under-utilized capacity. Empirically and conceptually, both sets of issues were very inadequately defined.

Third, and again related, were the distributional impacts of such a programme between and within countries of the South but, especially from OECD's own point of view, between and within the industrial countries of OECD itself. A major criticism of massive transfers was that its benefits would primarily accrue within the North to West Germany and Japan, thereby exacerbating the imbalances of trade which were already large and growing within OECD.

Finally, the distributional impact within countries was critical: indeed, it would be the main determinant of which groups would gain and which would lose from any initiative. Given extensive under-utilization of resources within OECD, it was not difficult to argue that the opportunity cost of many of the resources called into play by an increase in transfers would be low or even zero. As a whole, therefore, the programme was an excellent example of a positive sum game, in the mutual interests of both North and South. But positive sum games for a country do not mean gains for all parties within the country — which meant that clarifying the likely distributional impact was a vital part of the analysis.

However critical these four aspects, theory and analysis were inconclusive, deficient or silent on all of them.

(c) Or was theory simply irrelevant?

And yet ultimately one must ask whether it was the theory or the vision and the determination to act which was the real obstacle. When there is a commitment to act — as with the Marshall Plan some 30 years earlier — a sequence of actions can be set in train in which the interests of the main parties are taken into account in the working out of the initiative and the specific policies to implement it. This could have been done — and could still be done — with a massive transfer of resources in support of structural change. Its size, scope and sectoral coverage, the distribution of its impact across countries, in terms of where the resources are raised and of which countries or sectors will benefit, are all matters amenable to influence and decision in the way the initiative is developed or implemented.

If the will is lacking, such points become insuperable obstacles, not to be passed until every eventuality has been clarified and weighed, which can never be done. When, for some reason, the prize to be grasped is valued more highly, the obstacles and uncertainties are tackled with a view to getting them out of the way.

In the case in question, I was told in a well-informed interview shortly before the Bonn Summit: "These are not times when any Western Leader is looking for major international initiatives."

But why not? Is it "leadership" that is lacking or is it the leaders' inadequate perceptions of the issues and possibilities? And if the latter is the problem, is it not again a question of inadequate theory?

Chapter 10

Towards a Political Economy of the New International Economic Order

Alfred Maizels

The continuing *impasse* in North-South negotiations on the establishment of the New International Economic Order (NIEO) reflects essentially the divergent views held by the two sides of the debate on the nature and functioning of the present international economic system. These divergent views rest ultimately on the neoclassical economic theory underlying the attitudes of developed market-economy governments, and on the dominance/dependence paradigm generally accepted by representatives of the developing countries. Neoclassical economic theory tends to be invoked by developed market-economy countries to oppose intervention in the "normal working of market forces", whereas developing countries continue to press for regulation of market forces so as to provide greater support for the development process.

According to neoclassical theory, increased regulation of markets would add to existing market "imperfections", and would thus conflict with the argument that world welfare is maximized by non-interference in the free play of market forces. The question is whether the neoclassical approach is a credible one, in the light of the great changes that have occurred in the world economy since the end of the Second World War, and particularly the dominant market power that has come to be exercised by oligopolistic transnational corporations, and the widening gap between income levels in the developed countries and those in the majority of developing countries.

A valid theory of international economic exchange, particularly one involving the external relations of developing countries, needs to provide a credible explanation of the actual problems of development in the context of the economic relations between developing and developed countries, and also to serve as a reliable guide to effective remedial policies. On both these counts, neoclassical economic theory has become increasingly open to question.

The first section of this paper considers some of the principal limitations of the neoclassical approach to the development problems of underdeveloped countries, and concludes that the traditional neoclassical theory has little relevance to the understanding of these problems. This is mainly because it ignores both the historical background of underdevelopment and the influence of the existing institutional framework governing economic relations between developed and underdeveloped countries. This makes it particularly ill-suited to serve as a guide to policy on the NIEO proposals, which relate essentially to restructuring the institutional framework so as to ensure that the international economic system will provide far greater support than it now does for the development of Third World countries.

The second section then examines the arguments put forward in recent negotiations on some of the principal NIEO proposals. It concludes that, although traditional neoclassical arguments are frequently deployed by representatives of developed market-economy countries, their underlying objective would appear to be to retain effective control over the functioning of the international economic system.

A final section considers briefly some implications of the NIEO negotiations, particularly for a broader and more realistic theoretical approach to North-South issues.

The limitations of neoclassical theory

Traditional neoclassical theory proceeds from assumptions — full employment, perfect competition in both goods and factor markets, perfect factor mobility and price flexibility, and absence of significant "externalities", among others — which define an idealized market in which buyers and sellers trade in order to maximize their subjective utilities, while each factor is remunerated according to its marginal productivity. In such a perfect market the forces of supply and demand will produce, according to neoclassical theory, a rational price and income system and an optimum allocation of resources. Market "imperfections", such as oligopoly or "externalities", are then analyzed as aberrations from the ideal world of perfect competition. A separate branch of neoclassical theory has been developed to deal with international trade — since here factor mobility cannot necessarily be assumed — deriving from Ricardo's celebrated Law of Comparative Advantage.

However, the actual economic relationships between developed and developing countries are far removed from the idealized constructs of neoclassical theory, even when they allow for market "imperfections".[1] On closer analysis, "imperfections" such as oligopoly, "externalities" or State intervention are seen to be integral parts of the economic system, reflecting essentially the underlying power structure and its institutional manifestations. By regarding "imperfections" as aberrations from perfect competition, neoclassical theory implies that actual markets enjoy most, if not all, of the virtues of the idealized market, including an optimum use of resources. But, in fact, actual markets perform inefficiently in many important respects, not least in their allocation of resources. Particularly when the "free play of market forces" gives rise to large price fluctuations, the price mechanism fails to provide a sure guide to new investment and to rational resource allocation.

In the wider plans of resource allocation between developed and developing countries, the division of labour in which the majority of developing countries continue to export food and raw materials to the developed countries in exchange for manufactured goods cannot properly be understood outside its historical context. This "vertical" division of labour is a legacy of the Colonial period, during which the economies of the present developing countries were specifically moulded to serve the needs of the metropolitan powers. Indeed, the function of the developing countries as providers of cheap primary commodities was historically an essential element in the economic expansion of the present developed countries. This function can hardly be regarded as a viable basis for a genuine development process in the former Colonial territories.

Neoclassical theory does indeed allow for shifts in the international division of labour as a result of changes in comparative advantage, these shifts reflecting the movement of resources to (or away from) activities in which countries have a comparative advantage (or disadvantage). However, a characteristic feature of developing countries is precisely their minimal capacity to adjust their domestic resource allocations to suit changing conditions on the world market. Many such countries lack an adequate economic infrastructure to facilitate the redeployment of resources, while there may be difficult technical obstacles to overcome. A more pervasive factor is that existing social structures are often hindrances to efficient use of resources, as well as being instrumental in perpetuating great inequalities in living standards among different social and other groups.

Exchange between developed and developing countries does not consist solely of an exchange of goods. In fact, there is very considerable freedom of capital movement, and there have been large migrations of population between the two groups of countries. Given international mobility of factors of production, neoclassical theory demonstrates that, as a result of trade, countries will attract factors in which they are relatively deficient, and will lose factors of which they have a relative abundance. One would therefore expect to find a net flow of capital — both of human skills and of inanimate assets — from developed to developing countries, with a reverse flow of unskilled labour.

In fact, the net flow of capital is from developing to developed areas.[2] This is clearly the case as regards human skills (the "brain drain"). It would also appear to be so for financial flows, if one offsets against the flow from developed to developing countries the reverse flow of profits, interest and dividends, as well as the investments made by the social elites of developing countries in financial assets and real estate in developed countries.

Over the post-war period there have been significant movements of unskilled and semi-skilled labour from some developing to some developed countries (e.g., Mexico to the USA, Turkey and Yugoslavia to the Federal Republic of Germany), but in recent years restrictions on free immigration from developing countries have been generally tightened in virtually all developed countries. It would seem that, in general, both the unskilled/semi-skilled and the professionally skilled groups, as well as financial assets, are attracted to high income/high profitability areas, irrespective of their relative scarcity or abundance in their countries of origin.

The neoclassical approach also contains an important implicit assumption, namely that the existing distribution of incomes — among individuals and social groups within each country, and between developed and developing countries — can be taken as given. That income distribution is associated with a particular pattern of demand which — it can be shown by neoclassical theory — is best served by the resource allocation arising from perfect competition and free trade. The efforts of the developing countries to industrialize and, in some cases, to achieve a more egalitarian society, however, introduce specifically social objectives which would necessarily involve drastic changes in domestic income distribution, just as their efforts to achieve a more equitable international order imply a drastic shift in the international distribution of income. Viewed in this wider perspective, the existing allocation of resources can hardly be regarded as optimal.

Moreover, the concept of perfect competition assumes the existence of large numbers of buyers and sellers, each of whom is unable to influence the market price. This basic assumption has become increasingly invalid over the post-war period, particularly as regards trade between developed and developing countries, with the "free play of market forces" becoming increasingly overshadowed by administered pricing arrangements effected through intra-firm transactions of transnational corporations, long-term contracts (particularly in minerals), and transactions of State trading enterprises. In many primary commodity markets, the "free" market accounts for only a small proportion of world trade. The process of price formation, affecting the terms of trade of developing countries, has thus become more a reflection of a bargaining process between the main actors — private enterprises and national States acting either as sovereign powers or through their own trading organizations — rather than the resultant of a myriad of individual decisions of independent buyers and sellers.

Finally, because of its ahistorical approach and of its focus on the idealized market in which both buyer and seller gain, neoclassical theory can throw little or no light on the phenomenon of dependency of developing countries on the economic (and often political) interests of the main developed countries. A whole school of thought, originating in the "dependencia" theories developed in Latin America, has grown up to analyze this "extroverted" style of development typical of a wide range of developing countries. Whether or not one accepts all the conclusions of this school, it would seem incontrovertible that the key manifestations of underdevelopment — mass poverty and malnutrition, grossly inadequate infrastructure, a lopsided economic structure, excessively dependent on primary commodity production, lack of necessary skills and great inequality of asset ownership and income — cannot be explained simply by wrong domestic policies. They are, rather, very largely the result of the way in which the economies of the developing countries have been integrated into the existing world economic system. On this great issue, neoclassical theory, by its very assumptions, can offer little of significance to our understanding.

Mutuality and conflict of interest in the North-South negotiations

A growing body of responsible opinion — epitomized in the recent Brandt Commission Report[3] — views the kind of institutional reform implied in the NIEO concept as being in the mutual interest of both developing and developed countries. As indicated earlier, to the extent that institutional reform would involve greater regulation of market forces, neoclassical theory would regard such reform as tending to reduce world welfare. These divergent analytical approaches can be traced in each of the principal issues involved in the North-South negotiations. The following sections consider four of these issues, namely, those related to world commodity markets, to the patterns of production and trade in manufactures, to the principles and rules governing international trade, and to the international monetary and financial system.

A. World commodity markets

The principal element in the NIEO resolutions[4] relating to commodity markets and trade was that market structures should be improved through international measures to stabilize prices of commodity exports of developing countries at "just and equitable" levels in real terms, to preserve the purchasing power of these exports, to improve the share of developing countries in the transport, marketing, distribution and processing of their primary commodities, and to improve the competitiveness of natural materials facing competition from synthetic substitutes.

Since the adoption of the Integrated Programme for Commodities (IPC) at UNCTAD IV in 1976,[5] negotiations have been in progress for the establishment of international agreements for eliminating excessive price fluctuations in a range of commodity markets, and for setting up a Common Fund to finance buffer stocks established as part of such agreements. Though the Common Fund is in the process of being established, progress in the individual commodity negotiations has been extremely protracted. Of the 14 commodities listed in the UNCTAD 1976 Programme which were not already covered by international agreements, for only one — natural rubber — had a new agreement been negotiated by mid-1980. Preparations for new agreements have reached an advanced stage for a further two commodities (jute and tea), but for the remaining 11 commodities, accounting in aggregate for 30 percent of exports of primary commodities, other than petroleum, from developing countries in 1978, the negotiations have made disappointing progress.

The difficulties experienced in negotiating price-stabilizing agreements would appear somewhat surprising if the argument that such agreements would be in the mutual interests of both developing and developed countries is accepted. As the recent Brandt Commission report has argued, unstable commodity prices generally have an adverse effect on innovation and on the improvement of productivity in developing countries, while making rational fiscal and economic planning much more difficult.[6] It could be argued also that fluctuations in commodity prices often result in misleading signals for investment decisions, and consequently to a waste of resources.

For developed countries, too, there are avoidable costs resulting from commodity price fluctuations: sudden jumps in commodity prices accentuate inflationary pressures, with consequent loss of output and employment following remedial disinflationary measures;[7] volatile markets for certain commodities force enterprises in developed countries to hold larger stocks then would otherwise be needed; while the adverse effect of price uncertainty on investment in new capacity and in productivity improvement is likely to lead in the future to shortages of a number of essential raw materials required by developed countries. Thus, international price-stabilizing agreements are likely to bring real benefits to developed countries and, in particular, to make the task of economic management less difficult.

Opposition to the conclusion of price-stabilizing agreements by certain developed country negotiators has, however, been strong on occasion. One reason is the belief that such agreements will eventually become a means for raising prices above the trend, though in practice this would not appear to be a likely outcome, since importing countries would have an equal say with exporters in determining revisions of agreed price ranges. For commodities with terminal markets, opposition to price-stabilizing agreements has also come from trading interests who fear that reduction in price fluctuations will reduce speculative activity and hence their own profits.[8]

Opposition by developed countries to any proposal for an agreement to raise prices has been, and continues to be, very strong. The arguments usually adduced are, first, that such agreements are in effect a disguised form of aid (which should, it is argued, rather be given directly) and, second, that raising prices above what they would have been without an agreement will result in a misallocation of resources. Price-raising agreements (such as, for example, the original International Coffee Agreement, 1962), supported by developed countries will certainly involve an element of aid. Similar manipulation of the market by producers alone would, however, reflect solely their oligopolistic market power. As regards the misallocation of resources, it is doubtful whether a valid *general* case can be made, since any misallocation resulting from a price-raising agreement would have to be compared with the misallocation that would have occurred as a result of price fluctuations and other manifestations of the "normal operation of market forces".

Price-raising is thus not seen by the developed countries as an area of "mutual interest", but essentially as an area where their interests tend to conflict with the interests of developing countries. The UNCTAD IV resolution on the Integrated Programme for Commodities, which was adopted by consensus, goes some way towards the NIEO objective of improving the real prices of certain commodities and the establishment of a link between the prices of commodity exports from developing countries and the prices of their imports from developed countries, by calling for "... negotiated price ranges, which would be periodically reviewed and appropriately revised, taking into account, *inter alia,* movements in prices of imported manufactured goods, exchange rates, production costs and world inflation, and levels of production and consumption".[9] It remains to be seen, however, whether any new international agreement established under the IPC in fact attains this particular NIEO objective.

In view of the strong opposition of developed countries to the concept of price-raising commodity agreements, it seems likely that future action on these lines will be sought through supply regulation schemes by producers' associations, rather than by the traditional type of producer/consumer agreement. If so, then there would seem to be an implicit consensus that price-raising actions by producers reflect an essentially conflictual situation. It could, of course, be further argued that this is a short-term view, since in the medium- and longer-term one effect of price-raising by developing country producers would almost certainly be an increase in demand for manufactured exports from developed countries.

When one turns to efforts to enhance the share of developing countries in the transport, marketing, distribution and processing of their commodity exports, conflict situations would seem to be fairly general, particularly where entrenched interests of transnational corporations are involved. As regards transport, shipping companies in developed market-economy countries have maintained their predominance in merchant shipping, in spite of their increasing inability to supply crews (a critical input), by the use of "flags of convenience", a practice that allows them to employ cheap labour from developing countries while retaining ownership and control in their own hands. A resolution, passed by majority vote at UNCTAD V, recognizing the principle of "equitable participation" by the shipping lines of all trading countries in the carriage of bulk cargoes in their foreign trade, and calling for studies of measures to increase the participation of shipping enterprises of developing countries in the transport of their own foreign trade, was voted against by all the developed market-economy countries.[10]

These countries — the traditional maritime nations — argue that measures which reserve any cargo for the shipping lines of individual trading countries would reduce flexibility in the world shipping market, and raise costs to the detriment of shippers of bulk commodities. However, it would seem that there are many routes over which bulk carriers trade in a regular and predictable manner, where the carriage — now effected largely by vessels owned or chartered by transnational corporations owning the cargo — could be shared between importing and exporting countries without loss of flexibility.

The international marketing and distribution of primary commodities is another important area in which transnational corporations operate. Their control of the market varies widely, however, from commodity to commodity. There are probably no cases of complete monopoly both in production and in marketing channels, though in a number of important markets a few large corporations control a high percentage of either production or exports of developing countries, as well as the principal transport and marketing channels.[11] There seems little doubt that the intermediate stages between production in developing countries and consumption in developed countries — and particularly the stages of marketing and distribution — can be relatively very profitable, and in many cases entry is difficult or restricted. This is especially the case where these intermediate stages are, in effect, operations within the same transnational corporations that control the foreign trade side of the market (as is the case for a number of minerals), or where terminal markets play a central role (as for cotton, cocoa and coffee).

Efforts by developing countries to enhance their participation in the marketing and distribution of their commodity exports can follow either of two lines. First, there may be the possibility of changing the existing "rules of the game" to allow, for example, developing country interests full membership of terminal markets, so that producers and consumers can renegotiate on an equal basis the regulations which govern market performance. Another possibility might be the negotiation by developed and developing countries of agreed principles and standards for use in long-term contracts (particularly important for minerals and metals), which otherwise tend to protect the interests of the stronger bargaining partners.[12] While this approach might well have some "mutual interest" appeal, specific action has yet to be taken on these lines.

The second approach — which would inevitably raise conflictual interest problems — would be for developing producing countries to take measures, preferably in common, to increase their direct participation in the international marketing and distribution system. A number of options may be open, ranging from supplementing to replacing the existing institutional arrangements, depending very largely on the market power that can effectively be mobilized by such common measures.

Thus, the various proposals associated with the NIEO in the commodities field reveal a complex interplay of mutuality and conflict of interest. Mutuality of interest is most apparent in proposals for price stabilization, though even here mutuality is intertwined with actual or perceived conflict of interest. The willingness of developed market-economy countries to negotiate price-stabilization agreements remains influenced to a substantial degree by trading lobbies, as well as by fears that such agreements might lead to pressure by producing countries to raise prices, or otherwise to reduce the degree of control of the commodity markets at present exercised by developed country interests.

As regards the other NIEO proposals in the commodity field, which generally involve market intervention, or other action to enhance the market power of developing countries, there remains strong opposition by the developed market-economy countries. The argument that such proposals, if implemented, would accelerate the development process and, as a result, bring benefits to the developed countries also, would appear to be heavily outweighed by the fear the latter countries have of a reduction in their present predominant role in the organization of world commodity markets and the probability that this in turn would lead to a reduction in their share of the benefits of world commodity production and trade.

B. Production and trade in manufactures

The Lima Target and related NIEO proposals for a substantial acceleration in the industrialization of the developing countries clearly imply major structural shifts in the patterns of world production and

176

trade in manufactured goods. In particular, a rapid increase in industrial capacity and in the availability for export of manufactured goods from developing countries would require a restructuring of the industrial sector of developed countries to accommodate a large expansion in imports from developing countries.

According to traditional neoclassical theory, there would be clear long-term gains for both developed and developing countries from such restructuring of world industrial production on the lines of dynamic comparative advantage. For the latter countries, an expansion in demand for their manufactured exports would serve to accelerate their industrialization process, a necessary (though not sufficient) condition for their economic and social development. For the developed countries, the short-term costs of phasing out the less-efficient lines of manufacture would be more than offset by the longer-term benefits from increased activities — particularly from the high-technology and research-intensive ones — in which they have a comparative advantage and in which productivity is likely to grow at a faster rate than the average. Consumers in these countries would benefit more directly from access to lower-cost imports of a growing range of manufactures. There would be increasing potential for intra-industry specialization in trade between developed and developing countries, a process which could generate a substantial expansion in this flow of trade. Moreover, an acceleration in the rate of industrial growth in developing countries will inevitably result in higher growth rates in demand for the capital goods, technology, and associated services of the developed countries.

The case for world industrial restructuring on these lines in the mutual interests of both developed and developing countries is well known and appears to be widely accepted. The interesting question is why this case is unacceptable in practice to developed country governments, as evidenced by recent trends towards protectionism in the form of "voluntary" export restraints, "reference" prices, "orderly marketing arrangements", etc. directed essentially at limiting manufactured imports from developing countries. It is not that developed country decision-makers are unaware of the precepts of neoclassical theory; rather, that they are prepared to forgo long-term economic gains if they can thereby minimize short-term domestic political pressures. This they can most readily achieve by restricting imports from countries with relatively weak retaliatory power (i.e., the developing countries). Both the new forms of non-tariff barriers to imports, and the failure of the GATT multilateral trade negotiations to bring tangible trade benefits to developing countries, reflect essentially the lack of effective bargaining power of the developing countries. As a result, a disproportionate part of the burden of adjustment to the changes that have taken place in the world economy has been placed on the developing countries, which are least able to bear it.

C. The principles and rules governing international trade

Since the onset of the economic crisis in the mid-1970s, there has been growing awareness of the inadequacies of the existing principles and rules governing international trade, as embodied in the GATT. These principles and rules were drawn up, essentially by the main developed countries, at the Havana Conference of 1947/48. Since that time, profound changes have taken place in the world economy, as a result of which the existing principles and rules have become, to a greater or lesser extent, increasingly ineffective and outmoded. Here, it would seem, is an important area of mutual interest, in which a reformed framework of principles and rules could be negotiated. New or revised rules designed to protect the legitimate trade interests of developing countries, as well as to reduce trade barriers generally, would now seem urgently required in the interests of moving towards both a more equitable international trade regime, and a more efficiently functioning one.

Since the adoption of the NIEO resolutions in 1974, the demand of the developing countries for institutional reform in the field of international trade has widened from specific issues (e.g., implementation of a "standstill" on new trade barriers) to a general review and revision of the whole GATT system. It is now argued that the existing trading principles and rules constitute a central element in the inequitable and inefficient functioning of the international trading system, and that a fundamental reform is required to overcome their deficiencies. For one thing, it would seem anomalous that, whereas the principle of trade preferences for developing countries has been universally accepted, that principle is still treated as an exception to the trading rules rather than as an integral part of them. It could therefore be argued that the provision of a general legal basis for trade preferences for developing countries is now long overdue.

Second, the recent trend towards protectionism has used devices (such as the "voluntary" export restraints mentioned earlier) which fall outside the existing GATT rules, which are thus rendered ineffective as a means of restraining this trend. Unless such protectionist devices are brought within the scope of internationally agreed principles and rules (including provisions for phasing them out within a reasonable period), they are likely to have serious adverse consequences for the future of the world trading system.

Third, the growing proportion of world trade represented by the intrafirm and related-party transactions of transnational corporations also escape regulation by the existing trade rules. The trade of developing countries, in particular, has become substantially influenced by the decisions and practices of such corporations, which affect the location of production facilities as well as the volume, prices and patterns of trade flows. To be fully effective, internationally agreed principles and rules governing trade flows will need to be extended to cover the operations of transnationals.

Fourth, the principles and rules need to be extended to provide a suitable framework for promoting trade between socialist countries, which use state trading enterprises to conduct their foreign trade, and market-economy countries, where micro-decisions are usually taken by private firms within a governmentally determined macro-economic framework.

These and related considerations have prompted the Group of 77 developing countries to propose the convening in the early part of the 1980s of an International Trade Conference "to negotiate, on a universal basis, a new comprehensive set of rules and principles governing international trade relations...".[13]

While a revision of the existing trading principles and rules on the above lines would seem to promise advantages to both developing and developed countries, the issue also raises the possibility of a conflict of interest arising from differences in perception of the underlying problem. For the developing countries, the GATT system appears as one devised by the principal developed countries to safeguard their own trade interests, with relatively minor concessions to the trade needs of developing countries. A major revision and reform is thus required to ensure that the rules actively promote the development process, as well as providing an adequate framework for the smooth expansion of world trade as a whole.

For the principal developed market-economy countries, on the other hand, the GATT system is seen as having worked well over most of the post-war period, providing a framework within which an unprecedented expansion of the trade of these countries took place. The philosophy of the GATT system — based on reciprocity and non-discrimination — does not accord well, however, with that of non-reciprocal and preferential treatment for developing countries. The question is whether the two approaches can be combined into a single legal system, as envisaged by the developing countries, or whether the primacy of the non-discrimination philosophy is to be maintained. This latter approach, which has been strongly supported by the principal developed market-economy countries, envisages preferences for developing countries as a temporary expedient, which would no longer be granted when developing countries "graduate" to a level of economic development corresponding to that of developed countries.

Another major difference in approach, reflecting a more fundamental conflict of interest, relates to the nature of the future evolution of the world trading system. The GATT system was designed to provide optimum conditions for the "free play of market forces". However, as indicated earlier, an important part — possibly the major part — of the post-war expansion in trade engendered by the GATT system reflected the rapidly growing market power of oligopolistic transnational corporations. These corporations have also come to control a substantial proportion of the trade of developing countries. Hence, a reformulation of the trading rules designed, among other things, to regulate the trading activities of the transnational corporations would thereby introduce an element of global management, allowing the international community to exercise a significant influence on the pattern of world trade, as well as on the division of the benefits of trade.

One lesson that can be drawn from post-war developments is that the "free play of market forces" does not generally operate to accelerate the development process; rather, it tends to operate to provide a disproportionate share of the benefits of trade to the economically stronger trading partners (especially the transnational corporations). The question is whether, and to what extent, the developed market-economy countries will accept the need for regulating the activities of their transnational corporations, even though this is likely to involve a reduced share of the benefits of trade and a reduced role in the effective control of the trading system as a whole.

D. Reform of the international monetary and financial system

The reform of the international monetary system constituted a major element of the NIEO resolutions.[14] The NIEO proposals covered not only the reform of the international monetary system, including improvements in IMF financing facilities, but also the mitigation of the external debt problems of developing countries and assurance of flows of concessional finance.

As regards international monetary reform, the NIEO resolutions stressed a number of principles which should be followed: the prevention of the transference of inflation from developed to developing countries; the preservation of the real value of developing countries' currency reserves; the adequate, equitable and orderly creation of liquidity through the establishment of the SDR as the central reserve asset; the elimination of the instability of the system, in particular the uncertainty of exchange rate changes. In addition, the resolutions called for the early establishment of a link between SDRs and additional development financing, and for increased and more effective participation by developing countries in the decision-making process in the IMF and other international financial institutions.

Little, if any, progress has been achieved towards implementing these principles. An effective limitation of the transmission of inflation from developed to developing countries, as well as the maintenance of the real value of developing countries' reserves and the orderly creation of international liquidity, would all require, among other measures, a reduction in the reserve function of the dollar and the establishment of the SDR as the central reserve asset of the system — developments which now seem distant prospects. Furthermore, it remains to be seen whether the present regime of floating exchange rates will, in fact, reduce the instability of the system (even with the surveillance by the IMF over exchange rate policies that was initiated in 1978), while the proposal for a link between SDRs and additional development financing is still strongly resisted by some major developed countries.

Though the need for a reformed international monetary system is widely acknowledged, and indeed the main elements of a reform were elaborated some years ago by the IMF Committee of Twenty, the impetus for such reform seems to have been lost. Instead, *ad hoc* improvisations and makeshift arrangements have been adopted to meet particular disturbances, some of which are likely to impede, or postpone, the more fundamental reforms that are required.

As far as the developing countries are concerned, the operation of the international monetary system, as embodied in IMF rules and practices, has never served as an adequate support for their external financing problems. This inadequacy has become even more glaring with the sharp rise in the external payments deficits of the non-oil-exporting developing countries in recent years, resulting from the continuing recession and inflation in developed countries and the rise in oil prices. It is clear that most of the payments imbalances of these countries are structural in nature and are the result of changing circumstances external to their own economies. The IMF balance of payments support facilities, on the other hand, though they have been liberalized in recent years, are predicated on the assumption that payments imbalances arise essentially from inadequate or inappropriate domestic monetary and fiscal policies which, if altered in appropriate ways, will restore external equilibrium. IMF support facilities are therefore coupled with "conditionality" — ceilings and targets which generally tend to undermine development programmes rather than to assist in restoring external equilibrium with minimum disruption of the long-term development process.

A thoroughgoing reform of the international monetary system, with the objectives of providing fully adequate support for the external payments problems of developing countries, as well as promoting a much smoother international adjustment process, will require major changes in the existing principles of the system and in the operational rules of the IMF. It would seem that such changes are unlikely to come about without the full and effective participation of the developing countries in the decision-making process in the IMF. Voting power in the IMF, as well as in other international financial institutions, however, remains firmly tied to country quotas, which themselves reflect the relative national incomes of member countries, and a divorce of voting rights from financial power is likely to be strongly opposed by the main developed countries which at present effectively control these institutions.

The resistance of the developed countries to institutional change is also evident in regard to proposals to alleviate the debt burden of developing countries. These proposals were, first, that immediate debt relief should be provided, particularly for the least developed and the "most seriously affected" developing countries; and, second, that a multilateral framework should be established for future debt renegotiation which would operate on equitable and consistent principles designed not merely to resolve an immediate debt crisis, but rather to facilitate the resumption by the debtor country of its development path.

As regards the first proposal, a compromise agreement was reached in 1978 at the ministerial meeting of UNCTAD's Trade and Development Board, under which developed donor countries accepted a general obligation to improve retrospectively the terms of ODA debt in favour of the poorer developing countries, though they reserved the right to decide the modalities and the beneficiaries of their action at their own individual discretion. The measures taken as a result of this agreement have so far resulted in the cancellation (or refinancing on highly concessional terms) of more than $5 billion of ODA debt.

No agreement has yet been reached, however, on the second proposal, for a multilateral framework for debt renegotiation. An UNCTAD Intergovernmental Expert Group in 1976 reached agreement that international action on this issue "should enhance the development prospects of the debtor country...", but failed to agree on the appropriate institutional arrangements. The developing countries have proposed the establishment of an independent Debt Commission to analyze the development problems of debtor countries and to supervise the debt renegotiations. However, the developed countries have argued strongly that existing institutions, in particular the "Paris Club" and the World Bank consortia, would, with some modifications, be the most effective means for this purpose.

Finally, the various proposals — such as pledging of development assistance on a multi-year basis, and the imposition of an international development tax — elaborated in support of the NIEO call for more predictable and assured flows of concessional finance to developing countries have received little support from developed countries. A compromise agreement reached at UNCTAD V recommended that donor countries should announce annually their ODA plans or intentions for as long ahead as possible, and that UN development assistance organizations should try to achieve long-term finance, including multi-year pledges.[15] But the prospects for an international tax for financing development remain distant, and this may be due, at least in some degree, to the implications of such a tax for change in the present institutional arrangements for development assistance, which remain firmly in the control of the developed countries.

Some implications of the NIEO negotiations

It appears evident from the above discussion that each of the main issues involved in the NIEO approach to the development problem involves both mutual interest and divergent interest aspects, and that the two interact. Generally speaking, the mutual interest aspects of an issue tend to become relatively more prominent when improvements are being considered in the functioning of existing institutions. Examples of this would include the benefits for both developed and developing countries which could be derived from a reduction in protection, or from a "massive transfer" of financial resources to developing countries. On the other hand, where proposals for institutional change are concerned — and especially where these would result in more effective participation of developing countries in the management of the international economic system — then perceived conflict of interest tends to become the dominant feature.

Conflicts of interest arise on particular issues for a number of reasons. There are, for example, conflicts between sectional interests and, frequently also, between short-term and longer-term considerations. In addition, there is an underlying and more fundamental factor making for divergence of interest, namely, the need — as perceived by the principal developed market-economy countries — to preserve their traditional dominant role in the world economy by maintaining effective control of the key international economic and financial institutions, thus enabling them to determine the "rules of the game" governing international economic exchange. Since the NIEO proposals are concerned essentially with reforming the existing institutional framework of international economic relations, it is not surprising that they have made little headway, since they would involve a significant shift in the balance of control of the system.

A recent perceptive analysis by Hansen of the present stalemate in negotiations on NIEO issues identifies two principal reasons for the low priority given to such issues by the US Administration. One is the dominant view in the Administration that the existing international economic system does not require "structural reform" or alterations in the "rules of the game". The other is that NIEO issues are regarded essentially as peripheral to concerns of national security (or broad national) interest.[16]

In sum, it might be said that while the NIEO proposals for structural and institutional reform imply the existence of mutual interests, the scope for such reform is severely constrained by the fact that the present institutional framework reflects the existing power structure in the international economy, changes in which tend to be strongly resisted by the dominant economic interests of developed market-economy countries. As indicated earlier, proposals for institutional change which involve a significant reduction in the present degree of control by the developed market-economy countries over the working of the international economic system engender a fear by these countries that such change would reduce their share of the benefits derived therefrom. For this reason, above all, the developed market-economy countries have tended to relegate consideration of NIEO issues to a low position in their policy priorities, a tendency that has become accentuated with the deepening of the economic crisis in these countries and the consequent focus of policy on short-term economic problems.

A realistic theory of economic relations between developed and developing countries cannot therefore abstract from the institutional framework within which these relations operate. The nature of these institutions — the "rules of the game" governing international trade and financial flows, the degree and type of regulation of the market power of transnational corporations, etc. — are major forces influencing the division of the gains from trade and the style of the development process in the developing countries. Nor can a realistic theory assume that the process of price formation or changes in market shares necessarily reflect the free play of market forces. Rather, theory must take fully into account the major role now played by the relative bargaining power of the major actors in the development process, as well as their underlying mutuality and conflicts of interest, not only in the division of gains but also in the control of the economic system as a whole.

Notes

1 For a more detailed discussion of a number of the issues considered here, see G.K. Helleiner, "World Market Imperfections and the Developing Countries", in William R. Cline (ed.) *Policy Alternatives for a New International Economic Order,* Praeger, New York, 1979.
2 For a more detailed discussion of this point, see K. Griffin, *International Inequality and National Poverty,* Macmillan, London, 1978, pp. 26—35.
3 *North-South: A Programme for Survival,* Pan Books, 1980.
4 UN General Assembly resolutions 3201 and 3202 (S-VI) on the "Declaration" and the "Programme of Action" on the Establishment of a New International Economic Order.
5 UNCTAD resolution 93 (IV).
6 *North-South: A Programme for Survival, op. cit.,* Ch. 9.
7 For an analysis of the impact of commodity price rises on industrial activity in the developed countries, see Nicholas Kaldor, "Inflation and Recession in the World Economy", *Economic Journal,* 86, December 1976.
8 Such opposition appears to have been a significant factor in the long delay — over a decade — in negotiating the International Cocoa Agreement, 1972.

9 UNCTAD resolution 93 (IV), Section III, para. 2(c).

10 UNCTAD resolution 120 (V).

11 The data presented by G.K. Helleiner *(World Development,* 1978, Vol. 6, No. 4) on intra-firm transactions in US primary commodity imports, reveal a very high degree of control by transnational corporations in US imports of a number of important commodities exported by developing countries.

12 For further discussion of these issues, see *Marketing and distribution of primary commodities: areas for futher international cooperation* (TD/229/Supp. 3), Manila, May 1979.

13 Proposal submitted to the eleventh special session of the Trade and Development Board, March 1980 (see TD/B/791/Add.1, Annex I), and subsequently to the General Assembly.

14 See, in particular, A/RES/3202 (S-VI), Chapter II.

15 UNCTAD resolution 129 (V).

16 Roger D. Hansen, *Can the North-South impasse be overcome?* Overseas Development Council, Development Paper 27, Washington, November 1979.

List of participants

Valter Angell, Norwegian Institute of International Affairs, Norway.

Edmar L. Bacha, Pontificia Universidade Catolica do Rio de Janeiro, Brazil.

John Cuddy, UNCTAD/University of Geneva, Switzerland.

Carlos F. Díaz-Alejandro, Yale University, USA.

Ricardo Ffrench-Davis, CIEPLAN, Santiago, Chile.

Mahbub ul Haq, The World Bank, Washington, USA.

Per Haugestad, Ministry of Foreign Affairs, Norway.

Gerald K. Helleiner, University of Toronto, Canada.

Richard Jolly, IDS, University of Sussex, U.K.

Alfred Maizels, UNCTAD/University College, London, U.K.

Gerhard Meidell Gerhardsen, Norwegian School of Economics and Business Administration, Norway.

Ole Myrvoll, Norwegian School of Economics and Business Administration, Norway.

Gustav Ranis, Yale University, USA.

Stein Rossen, Chr. Michelsen's Institute, Norway.

Frances Stewart, Queen Elizabeth House, Oxford, U.K.

Paul Streeten, World Bank, Washington, USA.

Lance Taylor, Massachusetts Institute of Technology, USA.

Constantine Vaitsos, University of Athens, Greece.

John Williamson, Pontificia Universidade Catolica do Rio de Janeiro, Brazil.

Index

193